How to Get the Best Deal

Prentice Hall LIFE

If life is what you make it, then making it better starts here.

What we learn today can change our lives tomorrow. It can change our goals or change our minds; open up new opportunities or simply inspire us to make a difference. That's why we have created a new breed of books that do more to help you make more of *your* life.

Whether you want more confidence or less stress, a new skill or a different perspective, we've designed *Prentice Hall Life* books to help you to make a change for the better. Together with our authors we share a commitment to bring you the brightest ideas and best ways to manage your life, work and wealth.

In these pages we hope you'll find the ideas you need for the life *you* want. Go on, help yourself.

It's what you make it

* * *

How to Get the Best Deal

The savvy consumer's guide to
spending less and getting more

SUE HAYWARD

WARRINGTON BOROUGH COUNCIL	
34143100074416	
Bertrams	30/07/2009
AN	£9.99
STO	

Prentice Hall Life
is an imprint of

Harlow, England • London • New York • Boston • San Francisco • Toronto • Sydney • Singapore • Hong Kong
Tokyo • Seoul • Taipei • New Delhi • Cape Town • Madrid • Mexico City • Amsterdam • Munich • Paris • Milan

PEARSON EDUCATION LIMITED

Edinburgh Gate
Harlow CM20 2JE
Tel: +44 (0)1279 623623
Fax: +44 (0)1279 431059
Website: www.pearsoned.co.uk

First published in Great Britain in 2009

The right of Sue Hayward to be identified as author of this work has been asserted
by her in accordance with the Copyright, Designs and Patents Act 1988.

ISBN 978-0-273-72553-4

British Library Cataloguing-in-Publication Data
A catalogue record for this book is available from the British Library

Library of Congress Cataloging-in-Publication Data
Hayward, Sue, 1967–
    How to get the best deal : the savvy consumer's guide to spending less and getting
more / Sue Hayward
        p. cm.
    ISBN 978-0-273-72553-4 (pbk.)
 1.   Consumer education. 2.   Finance, Personal. I. Title.
    TX335.H385 2009
    640.73--dc22

                                                        2009021107

10 9 8 7 6 5 4 3 2 1
13 12 11 10 09

Cartoon illustrations by Kate Taylor
Typeset in 9.5/13pt IowanOldBT by 30
Printed and bound in Great Britain by Ashford Colour Press Ltd, Gosport, Hants

The publisher's policy is to use paper manufactured from sustainable forests.

Contents

To the people that matter most – my wonderful family
Mum & Dad
Barry & Millie
Roz, Steve, Amy & Natty

Acknowledgements

I can still see myself sitting in a BBC local radio studio watching the seconds count down on the clock before presenting my first live consumer programme. Producing the show, sitting opposite me, was my great friend Ant, who's still a great friend to this day. With just seconds to go until we went live at five past eleven, I remember saying, 'What happens if I can't speak once we're live on air?' To which he fell about laughing and just said, 'Physical impossibility Sue!' And, yes, we went live, the calls came in and a three-hour talk show seem to whizz past in a matter of seconds.

But what struck me from taking that very first call, as it still does to this day – whether I'm writing, presenting or being interviewed on consumer issues – is just how much we all want the best deal. Hardly surprising really; after all, nobody likes throwing money away. Yet we do, time and time again, through bad deals, not complaining when things go wrong, or just not knowing where to look for the best price.

Yet though I'd had the idea, this book didn't really take shape until last autumn when I got chatting to the lovely Elie Williams from Pearson Education. I'd actually rung Elie about a magazine feature I was writing, but we got chatting and when I mentioned my book idea, she immediately put me in touch with commissioning editor Rachael Stock, who within the space of a week had given it the thumbs up and suddenly it was all systems go on the writing front!

So huge thanks to both Elie and Rachael, whose enthusiasm and suggestions along the way have really helped shape the book.

And Elie has to get the credit for 'tweaking' and 'tightening' my version into the one you're reading now. As my husband Barry always says, I do have a habit of using fifty words when two will do! But what do you expect from a radio and telly type?

While much of the book is based on my experience and knowledge, I also enlisted the help of the wonderful Tony Northcott from the Trading Standards Institute, who proofread many of the chapters to check that any facts, figures and legislation were bang up to date, although inevitably over time rules and rates do, and will, change. So huge thanks to Tony.

To really bring the book to life I wanted to include lots of stories in it, in much the same way that people call into a radio show to share their experiences (all those *It happened to me* ones really did!). But there are also a number from other people I've met along the way who shared their experiences and let me put them into print, so huge thanks to them too.

Sue Hayward
April 2009

Introduction

How to get the best deal

We all love a bargain. We all like to think we're getting value for money, but chances are we often pay over the odds, or more than we need to, without realising. How many times have you sat next to someone on a plane and got chatting about the price you paid for your ticket? And when you find out they paid half the price you did – it hurts!

For some of us, being savvy with our money and keeping an eye out for the best deals comes out of necessity. If you're on a tight budget, looking for the cheapest offers is probably a way of life; it's something you need to do to avoid going into the red.

But the *cheapest* deal isn't necessarily the *best* deal; we get the two confused and this in itself means we waste money. Getting the best deal can mean the difference between buying something that costs just that little bit more but goes the distance, and buying something half the price that may only last a tenth of the time. Let me give you an example: say you buy T-shirts for your summer holiday; you can pick them up for around £1.99 (or possibly less with supermarket budget ranges), or you can spend £5–10 (or more) in many high-street stores. Go for the £1.99 'bargain' and chances are it may shrink and turn shapeless after a few workouts in the washing machine, whereas the more expensive version may look good and last the whole summer. So while in cash terms you saved a few quid buying the 'cheapest' one, was it really the *best deal*?

A big part of getting the best deal is about negotiation; or haggling for a better price. Now this doesn't mean asking for a discount every single time you buy something (I certainly don't go into Boots and ask for 20p off the price of my shampoo), but getting the best deal is about weighing up the situation and knowing *when* you're likely to get a favourable outcome and when you're not. Though once you know the basics you'll want to try it *every* time; believe me, a haggling success can be very addictive ...

When it comes to getting the best deal I learnt a lesson early on from a friend who worked in sales. 'You don't ask, you don't get' – and it's so true. It's unlikely that any company, store or service provider is actually going to voluntarily 'offer' you more for your money (unless they're struggling financially or trying to fight off their competitors), but if you *ask* you'll be surprised at how many of them will go that extra mile and agree a discount or price-match simply because you asked. I've been given a discount in some places, I'm sure, simply because they're so shocked that I've asked. Yet most Brits *hate* the idea of asking for money off; we fear people will think us cheapskates, rather than savvy shoppers.

Nobody likes getting a raw deal, but sometimes it happens; it's how you handle it that's important. How many times have you heard of someone having an awful meal in a restaurant yet not saying a word, even nodding profusely when asked if everything's OK, paying up and even *tipping* before moaning all the way home about the cold food and poor service? If we behave like this we've only got ourselves to blame. But chances are you can put it right and still get what you deserve, if you know how to go about it.

From tactics on how to ask for a discount in shops, to getting the best deal on a holiday and understanding your consumer rights, this book is about giving you the tools to be a more powerful consumer. It's about aiming for a five-star lifestyle without needing a six-figure salary.

It's also about knowing what to do if things do go wrong; say if you want to return something faulty or complain about bad service. Knowing how to make sure problems are resolved to your satisfaction is every bit as important as getting the best deal in the first place.

When money is tight, and even when it isn't, we can all get more from less cash if we know how to go about it. This book gives you all the tips and advice you need to get the best deal every time. Good luck and enjoy!

Part

The savvy consumer

Getting a good deal isn't down to luck. It's not something that happens by chance. You *may* get lucky and find what you want, at the price you want, simply by walking into the first shop you see. It *can* happen, but it's *unlikely* to happen and even more unlikely to happen every single time.

On the flip side, how many times have you snapped up 'a bargain' in that first shop, only to find it cheaper elsewhere or come across a better-quality version for the same price you paid?

Getting the best deal isn't just about looking at the price ticket. It's about attitude; it's about knowing what you want, being confident, open and approachable; it's also about mindset and believing 'I am a smart consumer and I'll get a good deal'. Say this to yourself and you'll be in the right frame of mind to ask for the best deal, and get it.

Let's go shopping …

How to be a cunning consumer

There are no two ways about it: businesses want your money. Being a cunning consumer is about spotting the tricks they use to persuade you to buy and spend more than you meant to, and knowing how to avoid them.

There's also no doubt that we want to spend, so it's just as important to understand the psychology of shopping and your own shopping personality. Finally, you need to get into the mindset of thinking about *why* you want what you want and how much are you willing to pay for it. Then you can learn where to look to find the best deals, discounts and promotions.

So this chapter's about being clever, knowing the tricks of the trade and becoming a truly savvy shopper.

Why we shop

Shopping is all about buying 'stuff'. Some stuff you need, like food, but what about the rest of the stuff? All those things we don't actually *need*, and often can't really afford? Like that new pair of shoes you'll probably rarely wear but felt you deserved after putting up with your grumpy boss all day.

There are, of course, any number of reasons why we shop: from being bored or fed up, to feeling happy or impulsive. Sometimes we can even shop as an alternative sport – long before internet shopping took, off mail-order companies always claimed to see a huge surge in orders (particularly from women) during the finals of major sporting events.

Then we'll go home and make excuses for our spending or even lie about the price of our purchases to our partners, parents or families to avoid one of those 'How much?' conversations. But what is it about *shopping* and *buying things* that keeps us going back for more?

The shopping 'buzz'

Psychologists claim one reason we shop is because we get addicted to the 'buzz' or high we get when buying something new. Just like a magpie seeing something sparkly, shiny and exciting, we spot that potential new purchase and want it.

Suzy Greaves, founder of the Big Leap Coaching Company, says it's down to brain chemistry. When we get that 'I want it' feeling and act on it, she says it releases a chemical in the brain called dopamine, one of your 'happy' hormones. This gives us an instant feel-good buzz, but it's only ever temporary; in some cases the feeling is over before you've even left the shop, or at best it can last a few hours until you're home. Once the effect is gone, and the eagerly purchased item has been relegated to the back of the nearest cupboard, we feel the need to go back for another 'hit'. And of course there's the 'down' side too. If you've spent more than you should have done, borrowed from the joint account or know you now can't clear your credit-card bill, this can bring you down even more quickly.

This craving of wanting to buy is, Suzy says, driven by the 'caveman' part of our brain. So whether it's a new pair of shoes, a car or a conservatory, that feeling of wanting something, fixating on it and hunting it down before buying, is due to an ancient part of our biological make-up.

Yet shop online and the hit is, naturally, not so great. Shopping online means a more measured, logical approach. We're less likely to give in to our emotions; hence doing the weekly supermarket shop online usually means a cheaper bill, as we're less likely to be influenced by our emotions the way we would be in the store.

Getting into the right mindset

You need to ask yourself if you're getting the best deal *every* time you pay for something. From your supermarket shopping to your holiday, from your mobile phone, gas, electric and car insurance to your bank account, a meal in a restaurant, to every bill that hits the mat. Think about what you're getting for your money and how much you're paying. Is there a better deal out there? And if so, how can you find it?

Get over your Britishness and try on 'front' for size

As a nation we feel very awkward about asking for a discount. In some cases we might actually think it's rude, or worry that we'll upset or offend people, or that they'll think we're tight or can't afford the ticket price. However, go to many other parts of the world and *not* haggling is considered most impolite and downright lunacy.

My belief has always been that my money's better off in my pocket than someone else's, so if I can negotiate on price, I will. So try on 'front' for size. Be assertive and learn how to ask for what you want without feeling embarrassed. (There's much more on this in Chapter 2.)

How the marketing people try to trick us ... and how to outwit them

Shopping is now seen as a regular weekend hobby and in some cases this has gone to a new extreme – think of the hordes outside Topshop when Kate Moss's range launched, or the stampede at Ikea in Edmonton on its opening night.

The marketing people behind those huge indoor shopping complexes aren't daft; nor are their counterparts who are working on encouraging you to buy their products and services. Everything from product slogans, TV commercials and magazine adverts, to the individual store layout is done to encourage us to buy more and spend more. And it works.

We've probably all been guilty of the odd 'impulse buy'. It's that magazine you pick up while waiting in the supermarket queue, a second lipstick because buying two means you get a free goodie bag, or sweets at the checkout to keep the kids quiet. But it all adds up and research shows that we each spend nearly £4,000 a year on impulse buys.

Stores also tap into our lust for the new. We are constantly bombarded with messages about things we have to have in order to improve our lives, and they fuel our desire to spend and buy more.

Here's how to outwit the stores and hang on to your money ...

Tricks to watch out for

Once you *know* the tricks the stores use to make you spend more, you can learn how to avoid them.

- *Eye candy* – the displays of magazines, sweets and chocolates at the supermarket tills – or tissues, batteries and travel-sized toiletries in the chemist, are all there to encourage us to buy.

- *Special offers and 'BOGOFs'* (buy one get one free) – these are packed onto the end aisles for maximum impact where you can't fail to notice them.

- *Being given a basket* – this makes it *so* much easier to buy more than just the two items you came in for.

- *Smells good* – coffee shops in bookshops are all about making you want to stay longer, so you perhaps enjoy a coffee while browsing the books, one of which hopefully you'll then buy. And in the supermarket the smell of freshly baked bread being pumped round the store means you'll feel hungry and probably grab a loaf on the way round.

- *Does my bum look big in this?* Tilted mirrors to make you look taller or slimmer, tinted mirrors to make you look tanned; all a sure-fire sales ploy to make you look and feel great so you'll buy.

- *Dynamic pricing* – this is marketing speak for chopping and changing prices, which means you'll pay more or less for something depending on where you live. In posh areas this may mean prices are higher, and city-centre outlets of the same chain will often charge more than the out-of-town superstore version for the same item.

Don't spend more buying special offers

Getting a discount or finding your favourite product on special offer means you've saved money, so don't fall into the trap of splurging what you've saved by buying a load of *extra* stuff that you don't need. Such is our genetic make-up that the 'feel-good' factor we get when bagging a bargain spills over. We get excited by the discount and spend more to prolong that shopping 'high'.

And are those 'three for two' deals really good value? What's the individual price of the item, and do you *really* need three of them or will two hit the bin unused or uneaten?

Be a cunning consumer in the supermarket

You can't see what's inside those packets and tins, so you plump for the yummy-looking picture on the box. Yet obviously you're not actually going to eat the box, so is it worth buying the most expensive brands just because you like what's on the outside?

While the packaging on the supermarkets' own ranges don't look great compared with the brand-name equivalent, you could be paying twice the price when you can't even taste the difference.

Swap brands

Try swapping your usual brand of beans, coffee, cereal or what-ever for the next cheapest one. If you don't notice the difference, stick with it. If you do, switch back to your usual brand. Turn it into a game and each week choose five items you can down-grade on; start with storecupboard staples such as spaghetti, rice, chopped tomatoes, kidney beans or tinned sweetcorn – don't tell your family and see if they notice.

In some cases you'll hate the cheaper version, but with others you won't notice any difference in taste, so they are well worth buying and saving yourself some money.

Eye level is 'buy' level

Supermarkets put their most expensive products at eye level as they're easier to spot. So if you're after those cheaper brands, look down – they'll be on the lower shelves, and the no frills and value ranges are usually hidden away on the shelves at the very bottom.

Headline-grabbing prices on the basics

In jargon terms they're known as KVIs: 'known value items'. These are your everyday basics such as bread, milk and eggs, and it's these items the supermarkets tend to compete on most. Their thinking is that if we find the cheapest supermarket for these, we'll automatically assume we're getting the best deal on everything else too. This is where comparison sites like www.mysupermarket.co.uk can save you money, because they price-match across several of the major supermarkets to find you the cheapest goods for your trolley load.

Steer clear of the middle

Supermarket layouts are pretty similar and well thought out. And that infuriating habit they have of moving everything around *just* when you knew where it was? Well, that's deliberate so you'll spend more time browsing rather than dashing in and out.

You'll find basics such as fruit and veg, meat, fish, bread and dairy products round the outside of the store, but all spaced out. Then you've got the buns, biscuits and all those tempting goodies slap-bang in the middle. What the supermarket's banking on is you walking through the middle, or at least up and down the aisles, randomly filling your trolley. So to beat them at their own game, stick to the edges for the essentials.

Shop just before closing

This is when you'll find all the reduced food that's got to be sold that day. For the best deals, go on a Sunday just before closing, or on weeknight evenings. Check the bargain bins for fish, meat, fruit and veg and ready-meals. Even if you can't use them that day you can freeze them for a meal next week.

Never shop when you're hungry

It sounds obvious, but shop when you're hungry and you're more likely to spend more. The reason being we get lured into impulse buys rather than just getting the basics that were on our list.

How to be a savvy consumer

This means finding the best deal and making it work for you. It's about knowing *where* to look – finding the places others don't know about – and knowing *when* to buy to get the best price.

Think outside the box

Getting the best deal isn't always about getting money off or the *cheapest* you can find – you should always weigh up what's the best deal for *you*.

Sometimes what you'll be offered in terms of extra service or added extras will be worth more in monetary terms than any cash discount on offer. If you're given the choice between having a free three-month extension to your gym membership (worth, say, £150) or £25 off the annual membership price, then unless you're planning to give up your membership in a year's time, the first one is likely to be the best deal. But if you've scrimped and saved to afford that membership, the £25 cash discount may well swing it for you.

Giving the customer more in the way of goods and services rather than discounting is usually a deliberate ploy on the part of the retailer. If companies can keep you as a customer or give you 'goods to the value' rather than lose cash from their till, they will.

Know when to shop for quality and when to shop for price

Sometimes you'll want something that will last for years and go the distance, so you'll be prepared to spend more. Other times you'll want something cheap and cheerful that does the job in the short term. There's no point spending a fortune on a top-of-the-range model if you're not going to get your money's worth from it, which is where the cost-per-use equation comes in.

I love this one as I've often used it with clothes usually to justify to myself why I've just spent rather too much money. Spending several hundred pounds on a suit might sound a lot of money, but if you're going to be wearing that suit to work every day, even within a year you're looking at a *cost per wear* of around a pound a day. While you could spend heaps more on a suit, at the other end of the scale you *could* probably find a more budget-priced one. But while this might do in the short term, chances are that, worn regularly, it's very unlikely to look as good long term or clean up as well, which could mean you may need several replacements over the course of a year. Just as with the scenario of buying those cheap and cheerful T-shirts for your summer holiday back at the beginning of the book, there are times when you'll need to decide whether your priority is quality and whether your decision is based on price alone.

Buy with selling in mind

This means buying items with a high resale value; something you need short term and can sell on afterwards, hopefully even for a profit.

This can be anything from tools and equipment needed for a DIY job (which may prove costly to hire if you need them for a couple of weeks), to clothes bought for a one-off special occasion that are unlikely to be used again. Some baby equipment, including buggies, baths, baby monitors and such like, you can practically get 'on loan', as you can easily recoup most of your money by selling them on later, providing the items are in good condition.

A savvy consumer's story

'I wouldn't normally dream of spending £130 on a high chair, but when I looked around I found there was a really good chance I could get back around £100 or more for a "Tripp Trapp" high chair by selling it on eBay. And it was the same story with other baby equipment, like the "Baby Bjorn 123" bouncy chairs and "Ergo" baby carriers, where you can recoup most of your money.

For this to really work you've got to do your homework carefully. Look at what top-end products are fetching secondhand, but what conditions are necessary to get that price, such as original packaging, etc.'

Naturally, nobody wants tatty secondhand baby gear, so only splash out on the higher-end products with a view to reselling *if* you think you'll realistically be able to keep them in good condition. I sold my daughter's baby listening monitors on eBay to a family in France for practically the same price I'd paid for them several years earlier. The trick? There wasn't one; just that the monitors really were 'as new' and a recognised brand from a reliable manufacturer.

If you're on a tight budget you may have to consider going for cheaper brands as there's no hard and fast guarantee as to exactly how much you'll recoup if you sell on. Yet if you go for the cheaper ranges, remember the resale value isn't as great because they're more easily affordable new.

So with a bit of careful shopping you can buy top-end goods that you couldn't usually afford, in the knowledge that you can recoup a big chunk of the initial value once they're no longer needed.

Pay cash not card

We think about how much we're spending much more if we pay with cash. Handing over a credit or debit card doesn't make us think about the price ticket in the same way.

Shop alone

We tend to spend more if we're with friends. Psychologists claim it's done subconsciously to maintain our 'self image'. Hands up those who aren't guilty of ever being encouraged to buy by a friend? Or spending just that little bit more that we know we should?

Save on delivery charges

Shopping online saves time but is it really good value when you add up all those delivery charges? It can prove expensive if you want a couple of items from several stores, so check delivery charges *before* shopping. This way you won't waste an hour on the site to find there's a £4.95 delivery charge.

Many stores do offer free delivery or there may be an easy way round it. If you're just a pound or two short of the 'free delivery', hunt round for another item you need or can make use of, to fill your basket, as spending another £2 to save a £5 delivery charge is worth it. But on the flip side, talking yourself into spending £10 just to get the free delivery isn't. Alternatively make a note of sites that offer free delivery and stick with those.

Buy show-home furniture

You can buy up the furniture that's been used for show homes at big reductions, simply because it's been on display. Ask the developer first to find out where they sell on, or go to discount warehouse outlets like www.showhomewarehouse.co.uk. Many high-street furniture stores such as Marks & Spencer, Laura Ashley, John Lewis and House of Fraser offload cancelled orders or surplus stock at out-of-the-way outlets like www.trade-secret.co.uk; they sell brand-name furniture at 50 per cent off the original price.

End-of-line, ex-display and refurbished electrical goods, like washing machines, laptops, dishwashers and plasma TVs, are often sold off on alternative websites. Comet, for example, sells new and slightly damaged products at up to 50 per cent discount at www.clearance-comet.co.uk. It is an auction site, so it's worth checking the eBay price first.

Buy trade

Lots of the DIY stores and kitchen and bathroom outlets offer trade discount. While you may not be 'trade' yourself, ask around among family and friends to find someone who's in the building trade or runs their own business and ask them to place an order for you to get a discount.

Buy out of season

Buying what everyone else wants at the same time means higher prices, as the shops know they can shift their stock.

Say you want a new bike, then the best time to buy is after the summer. Everyone's bought their bikes for the new school or university term and the Christmas selection won't yet have hit the shops, so you can find discounts.

Buy your tumble dryer in the middle of summer; or have your double glazing installed then. These aren't things you desperately need at this time of year, yet wait until winter and you may find it harder to get the best price.

Join the club

Sign up to free mailing lists with your favourite companies, including airlines, shops, hotels and restaurants, and you'll be ahead of the game when it comes to forthcoming sales, deals and discounts. One London boutique hotel regularly emails members with promotions, including selling off some £200 hotel rooms for £1.

Becoming a member means you'll get advance emails with discount vouchers or the option to book first when it comes to flight tickets and hotels. In some cases, depending on which company you 'join', you may have to pay a small fee, but if the discounts you'll get outweigh the initial fee, it's worth doing.

Befriend staff in your favourite store. If you're a regular customer they'll often put items aside for you or hold back sizes before they hit the shop floor. Of course they won't advertise this, but if you're a regular customer they'll often go the extra mile for you. I had a friend who regularly went to one particular clothes store; she was always very friendly with the staff and everyone knew her by name so they'd often save items in her size when they had a new delivery. Your own personal stylist for free, I guess, but this saved her the hassle of chasing around for a size they didn't have or had sold out of.

Some restaurant chains have their own loyalty scheme. Some are free to join; others you'll pay around £10 for a lifetime membership and you can get around 25 per cent off the bill during daytime and early evening.

Age-related discounts

It's not just students who can benefit from deals and discounts; hit the big '50' and there's lots of moneysaving deals, and it's the same for the over-sixties. Check out www.oscaruk.co.uk for deals for the over-fifties – everything from hotels, shopping, days out and financial products. And for the over-sixties, go to www.discount-age.co.uk. It is always worth checking the face-value price of any deal listed as *some* age-related offers may not offer the best value.

Money-off vouchers

Check out up-to-the-minute discounts at www.myvoucher-codes.co.uk. This is where you'll discover promotional discount codes offering up to 50 per cent off both on the high street and online. And if you find a money-off voucher for your favourite shop, chances are it has both a code for use online and a section to fill out to use it in store. Many vouchers last at least a month, so even after you've used the discount once, say in store, you can still get money off another purchase later in the month by using the promotional code online.

Price-match with 'shopbots'

Who has time to waste going from shop to shop comparing prices? Probably none of us, so use an online 'shopbot' (shopping robot) to do the work for you. Some of the major ones include: www.kelkoo.co.uk, www.pricerunner.co.uk, www.checkaprice.com and www.pricegrabber.com.

Tell the shopbot what you want and it compares prices across the board, flagging up both price and any delivery charge. It is worth checking a couple of shopbots as they don't all list every retailer, so you may find a deal on one that another can't match.

Eat out for less

Many top-price restaurants offer discounts if you pre-book or take advantage of 'early dining', typically up until 7.30pm. Check out www.5pm.co.uk for up to 50 per cent off restaurant menus nationwide or www.toptable.com for special offers. You can search by restaurant or by price and you can book up to six months in advance.

If you're a Tesco shopper, save your Clubcard points; exchanging them for vouchers against the cost of a meal out is worth it and you'll get four times the original value of your Clubcard points. So for every £5-worth of points you'll get £20 of vouchers.

Or you could become a 'mystery shopper' and eat for free. You'll get all your expenses covered but will usually need to answer a questionnaire or write a report on the standard of food and service after your visit. Doing a quick 'Google' search will bring up lots of companies doing this.

Cunning consumer nights out

- Love the theatre but find £50 a seat too much to pay? Try www.lastminute.com for special offers like tickets for a tenner to some of London's top shows. Tickets for Monday nights or midweek shows are usually cheaper than weekends.

- It's not quite a film première but you can get free cinema tickets to film previews, which is when the media go along to review the films! Contact www.seefilmfirst.com for details.

- Most TV companies also offer free tickets to show recordings; contact your favourite TV show for details or sign up on a site like www.bbc.co.uk/showsandtours.

Spread the word ...

You'd tell your friends about a great new restaurant, so why be shy about spilling the beans on how great your gym, bank or mobile phone company is?

'Introduce a friend' incentives are a cheap marketing tool. It's a low-cost way for companies to get potentially lucrative new business just for the price of a small reward to an existing happy customer. Depending on which company and service you're signing up to, you can get around £100 each, as many schemes pay both the *introducer* as well as the new customer – so you both come out better off!

Accept these for what they are; don't fall for the freebies in exchange for a product that's not right for you, or fail to read the terms and conditions.

How to negotiate on price (aka haggle)

We all want more for our money. If you've ever bagged a bargain or got a discount you'll know how good it feels, so why stop there? Why not get yourself in the habit of trying to get the best price you can *every* time?

Sounds a great idea, but in practice when it comes to asking for a discount, why do most of us feel embarrassed before we've started? We'd rather pay full price than risk being seen in public 'haggling'.

Yet transport us to a world of sun, sand and sea and most of us will have a go at (and even enjoy) bartering in the markets of Marrakech or the Egyptian souks. Not only can you pick up some great (and cheap) holiday souvenirs, but a bit of banter over the price turns into a right old game in these far-flung parts. In fact, offer to pay the asking price and you'll find the seller is downright disappointed, as 'haggling' is part and parcel of the culture. But while haggling (which basically means 'arguing' over the price) is acceptable behaviour abroad, how horribly distasteful and penny pinching can it feel once back in your own high street?

What you *should* be aiming for with your powers of negotiation is to be a shrewd and savvy consumer; so don't think 'haggle', think 'negotiate'.

Get over your discomfort and you'll often come away wealthier.

Think of negotiating as a game

While negotiating on price is about *what* you say, most of it's down to being confident and getting whoever's in charge of making the decision on your side. Keep reminding yourself it's a game, just like bartering abroad; treat it that way and it's easier to relax and enjoy the experience. And once you've clinched that deal or discount, I can't tell you how good that feeling is.

Chances are if you're out shopping you'll be tempted to blow any discount you've gained on an instant celebratory purchase, but even if you can't avoid that temptation, keep note of all the discounts and reductions you achieve to give you confidence along the way.

Now while this chapter mainly covers negotiating on price in stores, you can adopt the same techniques and principles with anything. So when you're looking to renew your car or house insurance, sign up for a gym membership, knock off the delivery charge for your new kitchen or agree a discount on your new business cards, be brave and have a go.

Where to start?

Think of the ticket price as an *invitation* to buy. The store is *inviting* you to buy yet legally it doesn't have to sell to you at all. Sounds a bit mad? Well, yes; imagine queuing up in a store only to find the assistant turns round, thanks you for queuing but says they don't want to sell the item to you today. *Unlikely* to happen, but under consumer law shops can refuse to take your money, although this part of the law is really in place to protect them from people who go in and make a nuisance of themselves or try to settle a £9.99 bill in pennies, or something equally daft.

So if the ticket price is merely an invitation to buy, you don't have to offer the full price – hence the opportunity for some serious negotiation.

A savvy consumer's story

Here's a great example of how a friendly and approachable attitude can get you what you want.

'When my husband and I were engagement ring shopping the only ring I liked was about four times our budget – typical. We looked around in other places but my heart was set on it. So we went back to the posh shop with sparkly windows and had a chat with the lovely salesman.

When we'd seen him before we'd built up a great rapport (he was Australian so we'd duly teased him about the cricket, at which we were, for once, soundly beating them).

We explained our predicament, and it turned out that the stone in the middle of the ring was some super duper diamond, very rare, etc. Well, frankly, you could put a bit of cut glass in there and I wouldn't notice, so he offered to replace it with a lesser (though to my eyes still gorgeous) diamond, which took it down to £500 over budget. We could live with that (just cut back on the wedding budget). Result.'

Don't negotiate in a hurry

Serious negotiation isn't something you can do in a hurry. That's where a lot of would-be bargain hunters go wrong – they give up if they can't get a discount within the first ten seconds. If getting a discount really was that easy nobody would ever pay the ticket price; we'd all be seasoned negotiators.

The general rule is: the more expensive the ticket price, the more time you're going to have to invest in your negotiations. So if you're shopping in a hurry, the kids are playing up or you're trying to beat the traffic warden back to your car, *don't do it* – you won't come across as being convincing.

Before you start, get into the habit of thinking about situations where you *could* conceivably ask for a discount. This can include buying something that's not perfect: a new jacket with a loose button, the last pair of boots in your size with a small fault. This gives you a good reason to ask for a discount.

Build up your confidence

When it comes to asking for a discount what's the *absolute* worst that can happen? Will you be thrown out of the store? Will there be an announcement over the Tannoy so everyone in the entire shop knows you've asked for a discount? Will warning lights go on every time you enter the store on future occasions? Of course not. At absolute worst the answer to your request for a discount will be 'no'. On occasions you may even find the store manager is more embarrassed refusing you a discount than you were plucking up the courage to ask in the first place.

And if there's no discount to be had, you've then got the choice of buying at the ticket price or walking away. Simple as that. So if that's the worst case, what have you got to lose? They're not going to put the price up, but they could put it down.

Keep remembering how much fun bartering abroad can be, and try to keep that sense of it being a game. It's a battle of wills, and how much better will you feel if you come away having spent that little bit less than the price on the tag?

If you really feel hesitant, build up your confidence by deliberately initiating a conversation with the cashier or assistant next time you go shopping. Get in the habit of doing this every time: whether it's the weather, what you're buying or how busy the store is – it will build up your confidence and make that next step easier. And if you're worried about being uncovered in the midst of your first-time negotiations by one of your neighbours or friends, put your new negotiating skills to the test in another town rather than your own back yard, so to speak.

A savvy consumer's story

Sometimes the first answer may not be the one you want, but persistence can pay off, as this story shows.

'I found a top I loved in the sale but it had two small holes in it. I asked the assistant if there were any more tops in the store, and there weren't. I said how much I *really* liked it but it had holes. "Oh dear", she said (helpful). The sale price was £50 (reduced from £70), so I asked if she could offer any more discount. "20 per cent", she said. I said I'd think about it.

I took it round the rest of the shop then went back to the counter and said, "If I don't buy this what's going to happen to it?" She said they'd probably throw it away. So I said, "Rather than throw it away, would you sell it to me for £20?" She went and asked her manager, who said yes. Hurrah! The holes were tiny and I've darned them, so you'd never know.'

Don't negotiate with the Saturday staff

You've psyched yourself up, practised your pitch and you're in the store, so chances are if you're the slightest bit nervous when you're approached by a sales assistant your carefully planned plea for a discount will come tumbling out.

Check who you're negotiating with; make sure it's someone with the authority to give a discount. Don't negotiate with the Saturday staff, however friendly and willing to help they are, as they just won't have the power to agree reductions. While it never hurts to chat to the assistant first and get them on your side, save your best negotiating tactics for the person who'll make the decision – usually the store manager.

If you've got a choice, you've got the advantage

If what you're buying is available from several outlets, think of it as holding the trump card. Most retailers will usually price-match if a competitor is selling the same item cheaper; although they won't always match online prices.

This way if you can't buy *what* you want at the *price* you want you'll have the confidence to walk away knowing you can try to negotiate further down the high street. Here's where doing your homework is essential as you'll be able to quote other prices or special promotions that competitors are offering; all of which strengthen your case for a discount.

Always ask for a discount on damaged goods

This is one of the best ways to get a discount. OK, so if you're buying something with your hard-earned cash most of us want the item to be in perfect condition; not something that looks like it's come from a car-boot sale or been in the loft for the past ten years.

Yet many stores will give you a discount simply because there's the smallest of faults or just because the item's been on display, but usually *only if you ask for it*. A 'fault' can be something as simple as the packaging being a bit tatty or dusty, to a small scratch, dent, mark, a loose thread on an item of clothing or a nick on a piece of furniture. In some cases you can even haggle retrospectively. Let me give you an example.

Sue's savvy stories – it happened to me

Hubby and I spotted a funky new dining table and chairs in a shop in Manchester while on a weekend away. We went in, had a look and, knowing we could order online, placed the order once home.

Delivery day came. We got four perfect chairs and a table with a two big scratches on the top. One phone call later, they arranged a second delivery, claiming to have checked this version, but this one was also damaged with a big dent in the side. Third time lucky, the table was better but this time the legs had some small marks on them. I was on the verge on sending it back for a refund when the driver told me the company routinely offered up to 30 per cent discount on faulty goods. His advice was to keep the table and ask for discount. "But don't let them fob you off with anything small, go for at least 25 per cent", was his advice; so that's what I did. I actually got the 30 per cent discount and kept the table while the store saved themselves the hassle of forking out for a refund.

Five steps to a successful negotiation

So if there's something you really want, the best way to get it at a good price is to decide on a strategy before you start negotiating.

Step one: plan your approach

Make the decision to ask for a discount *before* reaching the till. Holding up the queue while the manager is called won't make you popular with other shoppers, and you may be refused simply because management won't want everyone in the queue overhearing your request for a discount in case they all ask for one.

If you're making a big purchase, like a washing machine, computer or bed, you need to do your homework first. Price-match so you know you're getting the best deal and find out if there's a delivery charge. Are there any added extras offered in the price? Not only will your decision be based on price, but it's often about how reputable the store is or its level of customer service. So for example you may want to buy the item from one particular store because you value its customer service, but the store down the road is selling it for £20 cheaper or offering free delivery. This is a good way to open up negotiation as you're demonstrating you're a loyal customer. You're keen to buy from them and offering them the chance to make a sale if they can price-match.

With smaller purchases, asking for a discount is often much more of an impulse decision; like finding a new handbag but it's the only one left with a mark on it. But whether it's a long-term planned negotiation or a quick impulsive one, decide before you get to the till. Always ask for the manager or whoever's in charge while you're still on the shop floor.

Where you are is important because smaller, independent stores (or markets) are often more receptive to negotiation as the person in store may well be the owner. Managers in big high-street stores usually have sales targets to meet, but as the money in the till doesn't go directly into their pockets they may have limited margins for discounting. Push that bit further, though, and they can often make a call to someone higher up the chain to authorise a bigger discount.

Try and negotiate when you buy online too. Again if it's a smaller retailer they may be more open to a price cut as every customer is important to them. Some even *expect* customers to ask for a discount, as the example below shows, and if you don't ask you won't get.

A savvy consumer's story

Don't stick to face-to-face negotiation – often a friendly email can work wonders with online companies.

'I was about to pay far too much for some lovely duvet covers (lovely, but expensive!) and thought it was worth a quick email to see if they'd budge on the price as it was a small online retailer. With online retailers I tend to personalise my emails, as you're likely to be talking to a human being who may even run the whole operation rather than a 'customer-service-call-centre-scripted person' – and it works.

I wrote saying how much I loved the covers and could they give me a discount for buying two? I got a lovely email back from the lady running the company offering me a 10 per cent discount. And all for a quick five-minute email.'

When you negotiate is also important. Pick your moment: not a busy Saturday or five minutes before closing, as even a manager who's usually happy to negotiate will often refuse you simply because they're pushed for time. If giving you £20 off is going to lose them five other customers who walk out because they can't get served, it's not worth their while to negotiate.

If you're buying a big-ticket item, wait for the end of the month; the reason being that the manager may need to meet sales targets and may be more receptive to your reduced offer towards the end of the month than at the start.

Step two: smile, flirt and get them on your side

Smile, flirt and be friendly, as you need to get people on your side; and that includes the first person you meet in store. This could be the most junior member of staff, who calls the manager for you, so don't underestimate the fact that they may give the manager a heads up on whether *they* like you or think you're a time waster.

Flirt a bit, if it's appropriate (and you're comfortable with this), and remember a bit of harmless banter can go a long way when it comes to negotiating a discount. So be friendly even while you're first looking at the item (all part of the build up) – look confident and interested.

Be firm as well as charming; sales people can tell if you're nervously trying it on, but if you show you mean business and are expecting a result by your confident manner and relaxed body language, you're more likely to get what you want.

Get them on your side; if the staff *like* you they'll want to help you, and if they've got the power and authority to give a discount, chances are they will. If, on the other hand, you're rude, surly and grumpy and demand a discount they may decide (despite having the power to authorise a discount) to stick with their ticket price.

Step three: be enthusiastic about what you're buying

Tell them how *much* you want it, *why* you want it and why you'd *really* like to buy it today, *from them*, rather than from their competitor down the road.

Give them a reason as to *why* you should get a discount. A straightfoward 'Can I have some discount?' is easier to refuse, whereas giving them a plausible reason to give you a discount leads to negotiation. It could be that the item is a display model, there's a mark on it or you're buying several items in store.

Or ask if they'll throw in free accessories: for example shoe polish if you're buying shoes or boots; a gift box for jewellery or cosmetics; make-up or perfume samples if you're buying the full-size version; or even spare batteries for a new camera.

Cash is king. The jury's still out on this one; in some cases offering to pay cash will be the deal clincher and will get you a discount, as accepting credit cards cost shops money. When paying for services, like car repairs, carpet fitting or a plumbing job, you'll usually always get a discount for cash as it means instant cash flow without them having to pay cheques into the bank. But in your typical high-street store, where they're geared up to take credit and debit cards, the offer of cash is usually unlikely to sway them.

What to say (the words and phrases to use)

Buying more than one of something

'I'd like to buy two (or three or more) of these; what's your best price if I buy both?'

Ask them to price-match

'I'd like to buy X from you but I've shopped around and found you're selling it at £50 more than X down the road/online. Can you price-match if I buy now?'

A discount for cash

'I'd like to buy X but £250 is more than my budget. Are you able to give me a discount for cash?'

Ask for something 'extra'

'Would you throw in some batteries/shoe polish/sample sizes too?'

Step four: how much discount to go for?

There are no set rules on this, but go in with too low an offer and you can find you're not taken seriously; ask for too little off and it's probably not worth your time negotiating.

Ideally, go in at around 60–70 per cent of the asking price; this paves the way for negotiation. So, say you're looking for a reduction on a £100 table with a small scratch on it, you could try going in at £60–65 with the realistic expectation that you can settle on, say, £75–80 for a final price. Remember that it's a game, so if you suggest a price, it's unlikely this will be accepted, as the manager won't want to lose face and may ask for more.

It's always worth opening up the negotiation yourself. If you ask what discount they'll offer and it's a measly £5 on the same £100 table, it's going to make your potential £60 offer look a bit of a joke.

Don't start negotiating unless you're serious about buying. I learnt my lesson the hard way after trying to knock down the price of a hand-carved nativity set for my mum and dad in Jerusalem a few years ago. Having fallen into negotiation with one store owner after casually asking the price, I then decided after closer examination that it wasn't carved as well as the one in the shop next door. So I left, went next door and cut a better deal there. End result: me and a friend being chased through the labyrinth of streets by a screaming shop owner. Thankfully, the nativity set (which my parents loved, so well worth the experience), the friend and I survived intact. Although shopping in the UK is not likely to have these kind of issues, there is however an expectation that if your request for a discount is met, you will go ahead and buy.

Step five: the deal is done

Once you've both agreed on a price, stick with it. At this point you shouldn't be unclear as to the terms of the discount or deal, but if you are, clarify by saying something like, 'So that's 20 per cent off if I buy now', or '10 per cent off because the box is damaged', so everyone's clear on what's agreed. This saves horrible embarrassment at the till if there's been a misunderstanding.

Warning! You can forfeit your rights by haggling

If you're negotiating money off because of a 'fault', you may find that once the deal's done you can't return the item for an exchange or refund.

Many high-street stores have very generous returns policies and will refund you simply because you've changed your mind, providing you've got the receipt, but if you've negotiated a discount on the item due to a fault, you often have to waive your right to a refund if you change your mind.

If, however, the item later develops *another* fault and it's not the one you were given a discount for, then you can still return the item as faulty for a refund, exchange or repair. Usually stores will explain all this to you when you agree a discount for damaged items, but if they don't, do ask.

When to walk away

If despite your best efforts to negotiate it's still a 'no go', be polite and walk away. Don't feel embarrassed or get stroppy. Think of it as their loss; as you'll be giving another store your money.

Walking away can also be a good tactic as if there's any last hope of the store caving in – it's at this point they may agree to the deal. This can be a real test of nerves to see who 'cracks' first; and if you really want something it's hard to keep on walking. But remember, if you do walk away you can always go back in the store and buy the item at the full price later that day if you don't want to lose face by immediately paying full price after being refused a discount. Obviously this isn't the same with some items, like, say, secondhand cars, which could well be sold by the time you return, so if you've walked away without being called back to agree the deal, it's down to you whether you return after a quick coffee break or not.

A savvy consumer's story

Negotiating can be a test of nerves, as this story shows

'I remember my dad coming with me to buy my first ever car (old and second-hand, but oh so wanted). My dad handled the negotiation and reached a point where he said, "No, sorry, if you can't move on price or even throw in car tax, we'll have to look elsewhere". He then turned and walked towards the garage gates. I followed, inwardly thinking "No Dad, I want it, and I'll pay that much as it's my money …", but luckily kept quiet and just followed. Just as we reached the final row of cars by the gate the salesman shouted after us, "Oh, I'm sorry, did you say six months tax? I thought you meant twelve". We got the car, with the tax we wanted.'

Lesson learned.

In some cases you may want time to think about the deal being offered, especially if you're buying a larger item. So if you're trying to sort out a new kitchen and are being offered a 20 per cent discount, ask for ten minutes to think about it or go for a coffee. Many large stores have their own coffee shops and this is an ideal place to go for a five-minute breather before you agree to a deal. If you're not confident with your mental arithmetic, always take a calculator so you can double check if the discount is as good as you think.

Beware any *instant deals* only available at that point in time. This is more the type of deal you'll be offered by a double-glazing company once their rep is sitting on your sofa and looking unlikely to move for the next five hours. If you're being offered a big discount that's only available at that point in time, walk away.

Get into the haggling habit

Although most of this chapter is about negotiating on price if you're buying in stores, you can adopt the same rules, techniques and principles when buying from other sources, such as online retailers, or negotiating deals on services.

Whenever any contract or subscription (be it your gym membership, car insurance or mobile phone contract) is up for renewal, you're in the best bargaining position. Most companies want to keep their customers, so if it means giving you a discount to stay, it's worth it. *But* they won't broadcast this or offer it; *you've got to ask.*

Tell them you're thinking of leaving, have another deal to quote to them and chances are they'll either discount your existing deal or offer you an upgrade or extension for the same, or a discounted, price. When negotiating renewal contracts by phone, say for mobile phones, broadband or insurance, a handy tip is to always ask for the disconnections department. They can authorise far bigger discounts than call-centre staff and it's ultimately their job to keep customers.

Decide upfront what you'd like and tell them. I call my mobile phone company every year before my contract ends and ask what they can do to keep me as a customer, and every year I'm offered a new handset (for free) and more inclusive minutes and texts – all for the same price as before. Yet they'd be unlikely to call me up *offering* a free upgraded phone as an incentive to stay with them; they'd rather wait until they think you're leaving to offer this. (There's lots more on how to negotiate on services like this in Chapter 6.)

It is always worth knowing that you stand to gain in situations like these; partly because companies don't want to lose customers, and partly because they make money from those customers who just automatically renew *without* trying to negotiate. So don't let them make money from you; be the one who gets the best deal.

How not to get ripped off

Unless you've got money to burn (which most of us don't), we naturally like to feel we're getting value for money and not being ripped off or sold short.

There's not much point congratulating yourself on negotiating a great price or deal if you leave yourself open to being ripped off.

Being ripped off, conned, scammed, or discovering you've paid over the odds is a horrible feeling and one that can have lasting repercussions, particularly if you've landed yourself in debt to pay the bill or, at worst, lost your life savings to a scam.

But being ripped off isn't just about falling victim to a dodgy cowboy company; you could be ripped off by your bank or credit card company simply because you didn't read the small print and ended up paying unnecessary charges.

This chapter is about being one step ahead every time, and how to spot those tricks, scams and charges before they hit you where it hurts – in your pocket.

Cowboy builders, dodgy plumbers and 'here today, gone tomorrow' block-paving companies

Even if you're *thinking* of having your driveway paved, bathroom painted, conservatory built or a carpet laid, don't give the job to anyone cold-calling at your front door. Chances are they'll be of the 'here today, gone tomorrow' school of traders and will want payment in cash upfront.

With your opportunist doorstep caller, the typical patter is often that they're working in the area, have got materials left over and conveniently noticed that your roof, drive or brickwork needs work doing. You'll probably get an instantly low quote but they'll want cash payment (upfront), and your only form of contact will often be nothing more than a mobile phone number.

If you want a job done, always contact tradespeople yourself for quotes. There are lots of ways to check a trader's credentials, so don't believe what they say just because they've got a business card or website. A business card could have totally bogus numbers and addresses, and websites are nothing more than pictures and words on the internet – very easy to set up if you know how.

If you're asked to pay up before a job's finished you should be sceptical and ask why. Any decent tradesperson will want to make sure you're happy *before* you hand over payment. Another well-known rip-off is the builder (or tradesperson) who comes in for one job and then finds a long list of other problems (usually on the roof or up in the loft where you can't see them) which 'really should be fixed', and of course they're available and willing to do the job for you at an inflated price.

Watch for the cheap quote that goes up (and up)

You get what looks like a cheap quote for the job, *much* cheaper than anyone else, so you go for it, but then the price goes up with lots of little extras, like the fact that disposing of all the debris and rubbish wasn't part of the deal so your friendly trader can take it to the dump but it'll cost you … Or the fact that they now need more materials to do the job, or it's taking longer than they thought, so you've got to pay another two days' labour. Or there's the one where they decide they need to bring along someone else to help them but, yes, you've guessed it, you're the one who'll pay the bill. This is why it's really important to ask lots of questions and try to cover every eventuality when you first agree the job.

There's lots of advice on how to check out tradespeople and garages, compare quotes, protect yourself and avoid being ripped off in Chapter 9 on small businesses, but it's also worth saying that there are some really good tradespeople out there and some of them get ripped off by customers who try to avoid paying up or attempt to get something for nothing.

Rip-off charges

Yes, these are those 'hard-to-spot' sneaky charges that get slapped onto your bill right at the end, so you often don't notice them before you pay.

Service charge in restaurants

While the charge itself isn't a rip-off, and is in fact probably very much deserved by the waiting staff who aren't paid big salaries, make sure you don't pay twice over. These days paying by debit card means you often get the option to add on a 'gratuity' charge. Don't be afraid to decline this option if either the service was poor – in which case you should have said something already – or the service charge has already been included in the bill.

And if the service charge hasn't been included and you do want to tip, do it in cash. One restaurant chain hit the headlines after it was found to be charging staff a fee to give them tips if customers had added them to the bill and paid by credit or debit card.

Hotel phone charges

These are hideously expensive as hotels whack on a hefty surcharge on top of the standard rate, which can be a truly frightening cost if you're calling from abroad. There's more on getting the best deals using your mobile abroad in Chapter 6, as this is often a far cheaper method than using the hotel phone.

All-inclusive prices that aren't

Whether it's holidays, all-you-can-eat buffets or prices for repairs, always check what's *not* included. There's lots more on holidays in Chapter 10, but be warned that some of those 'all-inclusive' holidays aren't what they seem. You may find, for example, that when it comes to ordering drinks you're restricted to the local beer and spirits for the inclusive price.

Many of the all-you-can-eat buffet-style restaurants have a fixed price for food only, so if you're on a budget watch the drinks' prices as these can bump up the bill a lot.

With repairs, if you're given a price for a call-out and, say, the first hour's labour, check the rate beyond that. What's the cost for every hour's work after the first hour and how accurately will the visit be timed? Is VAT included (if they're allowed to charge it) or will it be extra? There's lots more on this in the small business chapter further on (Chapter 9).

Protect yourself from bank fraud

This is a *huge* problem and one of the biggest rip-offs out there. Credit and debit card fraud costs the UK millions of pounds every year. And it's on the rise. Identity theft – stealing someone's name and address and getting cards, loans and mortgages in their name – is now the UK's fastest growing crime. So how can you make sure it doesn't happen to you?

Check your bank and credit card statements

Don't rip open the thing, give it a cursory glance and chuck it in the nearest bin or, worse still, leave it unopened in a drawer for six months. Get in the habit of checking your statements every month. Look for any transactions you don't recognise, and if there's a payment you're unsure about, call your bank or card company who will investigate it for you.

Even in genuine cases, some payments you've made, for example at your local petrol station or with an online company, can sometimes appear under an unexpected name, like the company's parent group or a different trading name. For this reason you should always hang on to all your receipts so you can cross-check payments every month. If you ask for a payment to be queried, your bank or card company will usually temporarily suspend the payment while they investigate it, but even if the transaction is found to be genuine you won't be charged for the bank's time, so never be afraid to ask if you spot something you don't recognise.

Don't duplicate PIN numbers and passwords

How many of us regularly use our date of birth as our PIN (personal identification number) or the same password on not one but *all* our online accounts, simply because it's easy to remember? While this may make life simpler for you, using the same PIN or password for all your accounts could prove costly if your card is used fraudulently.

Under the Banking Code banks will cover the cost of any loss you incur through fraud, but *only* if you acted responsibly with your cards. Writing down PINs or passwords, keeping a note of them in your wallet or handbag, or using the same code for all your cards *could* be considered irresponsible, leaving you potentially at risk of covering the cost of any losses. And it's the same with online or phone banking; using your pet's name or mother's maiden name as the password on an account is easy to remember, but easy too for fraudsters to find if they've gone through your bin and picked up your personal rubbish. Ideally a password using a mix of letters and numbers is harder to crack. For a quick test on how easy it is to crack your password, go to www.passwordstrength.net, which measures how secure it's likely to be, depending on the combination of letters and numbers you've used.

Protect online accounts

Fifteen million of us regularly use the internet to check our bank accounts, according to the banking organisation APACS (Association for Payment Clearing Services) And banks are advising customers to ensure they've got up-to-date anti-virus systems and firewalls on their computers when accessing accounts. If you don't, you *could* be liable if accounts are hacked into, as banks could claim you were negligent or acted irresponsibly. Don't use public computers in libraries or internet cafés to access bank accounts and always log out at the end of each session so that your account isn't live, otherwise other people can access it using the same computer.

Fraud-buster tips

- Check nobody can see you enter your PIN at cash machines.

- Watch out for 'skimming'; this is when your card is copied and the copy card is used to raid your account. It can be done when your card is swiped, so don't let your card out of your sight, particularly when abroad.

- Check cash machines before using them; 'skimming' devices often stick out beyond the card slot and if you spot anything suspicious, don't use the machine – report it to the bank immediately.

- Even leaving your credit card behind a pub bar to 'run a tab' could be deemed 'irresponsible' and mean you're liable for any financial losses incurred, so hang on to your cards. If the pub wants your card, settle your bill as you go.

- If you're called by your 'bank', don't give out personal details over the phone. Call them back on the number printed on your statement.

- Shred everything with personal information on it, including bank account details and credit card numbers.

- Remember to log out after accessing online accounts, particularly on public computers in libraries or internet cafés.

- Cut up old debit or credit cards, going through the magnetic strip, and call your bank to close down the accounts and to ask for written confirmation when this is done.

- If you've been a victim of card fraud, contact your bank immediately.

Spending abroad – credit card rip-offs

Taking your plastic on holiday is easy and convenient. There's no problem exchanging traveller's cheques or carrying heaps of

cash, but always take more than one card with you, ideally from a different provider, in case your bank stops your card due to anti-fraud measures. This isn't so much about being ripped off, as the bank's anti-fraud measures should protect against this, but it's about not being caught short.

Basically banks use special anti-fraud systems to monitor customers' spending habits, including where, when and how frequently we use our cards; so if they suddenly discover you're spending a few thousand baht in a shop in Thailand, when you don't usually venture further than your nearest town, they *may* reject the transaction. In practice this means your UK card issuer will need to speak to you directly to verify the transaction, but if your card company doesn't have your current mobile number, or your phone's switched off, the transaction will automatically be refused.

So don't rely on just one card abroad, take a couple, as different companies have different systems in place to pick up on unusual spending patterns. Some card providers suggest you call them before travelling abroad, telling them where and when you're going. However, I'd advise against giving such detailed information as if it falls into the wrong hands someone will know when you're out of the country and that your house will be empty for two weeks! Although the banks deny this could happen, there have been several documentaries showing reporters infiltrating call centres and coming away with customers' personal details, so just tell your card company the countries you're likely to be visiting over the next few months.

Don't withdraw cash on your credit card

It's expensive, so don't do it. Use your card for purchases rather than cash withdrawals. Taking out cash on your card costs around £1.50 a time, plus you'll be charged interest on the money from the day you withdraw it and the rate's higher with cash withdrawals than purchases. Use your card for payment only and don't rely on it for cash.

Pay in the local currency

We probably all try to convert the currency into pounds sterling in our heads, but after a few glasses of wine at the local taverna it can be even more tricky. So if you're offered what looks like an easy option to have your Thai baht, euros or Swiss francs converted to a currency you're more familiar with – pounds sterling – many of us would be tempted to go for it, but *don't do it!*

Dynamic currency conversion, or DCC as it's known, is costly. We throw away £70 million a year in unnecessary costs having local currency turned to pounds before settling the bill on holiday. While it sounds an easy option, the catch is that the conversion rate is usually decided by the retailer, who may also add on a service fee.

While paying in the local currency can incur fees from your UK card company (known as a 'loading' fee when they convert from one currency to another), there are several cards on the market that don't impose these charges.

Sue's savvy stories – it happened to me

When you're abroad it's easy to get ripped off simply because you're unfamiliar with the currency, so it is worth keeping big notes well away from your small change.

I remember a rather expensive taxi ride in Istanbul when one of our group overpaid the driver by the best part of £50 for what was in effect a £4 taxi fare. After getting out, one guy handed over a note and the driver rather rapidly sped away without offering any change. As our friend thought he'd only handed over a couple of pounds as a tip, he wasn't worried about the

lack of change, until he realised he'd muddled up the notes and been rather too generous by giving the driver the equivalent of £50 instead of £5.

Scams and other rip-offs to watch out for

Over three million of us fall victim to scams every year, collectively losing over three billion pounds, according to figures from the Office of Fair Trading. So what should you watch for and how can you protect yourself?

Timeshare and holiday companies

If you've ever taken a trip to Spain you'll know how annoying timeshare touts can be. Just like flies buzzing round you, bat one away and you'll find there are another couple ready and waiting to pounce! But while hearing the word 'timeshare' may be enough to put most people on their guard, some holiday companies are now getting more slick and practised at wrapping up the concept. This may mean being offered a free luxury break, but the reality often means wasting several hours, if not days, of your trip experiencing timeshare presentations with a hard sell at the end.

Abroad, the typical 'patter' starts on the street, when you're suddenly 'befriended' by a stranger offering prizes if you attend a short 'holiday' presentation. Transport and drinks are usually thrown in to entice you along and, once there, after a guided tour of the complex, you'll face a hard sell by the timeshare company. I sat through one of these once, just for the experience, in Lanzarote, and it wasn't enjoyable. Bearing in mind you're whisked off in a taxi to a building site in the middle of nowhere, you've lost your bearings already, which can make getting back to your hotel tricky as you're dependent on finding a cab. Then you've got the hard sell, and even when pleading complete poverty (which was my excuse in the end), they'll still find a way to try to persuade you to sign up, even for the smallest amount.

It is worth remembering that a bona fide company won't pile on the pressure to get your money before you leave the resort; their deal will still be available when you get home.

How to handle this one? Just say no and walk away; don't go along, however tempting the promise of free gifts, prizes or free drinks may sound. Any 'short' presentation will turn into several hours of your holiday; and they won't be keen to let you go.

How to get out of it

If you sign up and regret it, contact the Resort Development Organisation (www.rdo.org), as you have a ten-day cooling-off period when buying in Europe or fourteen days if the contract was signed in the UK.

While the Timeshare Act of 1992 does protect consumers, there are several exclusions from the ten-day cooling off period, including buying into holiday or vacation club schemes, time-shares on boats and timeshares lasting less than three years.

Phone slamming

This is when a rogue phone company tries to switch you over to its service without your say so, and currently Ofcom, the telecoms regulator, receive over seven thousand complaints a year about this.

Strange as it sounds, these rogue companies don't need your signature or bank details to initiate a switch; your postcode and home phone number is enough to start the wheels in motion. Usually the first sign that something's up is when you open a 'sorry to lose you' letter from your existing provider. If you don't act quickly it could mean you end up being switched to another company, who will then start billing you for any phone calls you make.

How to get out of it

Contact your current supplier immediately. They may be able to block the switch as there's a ten-day period before the account can be transferred. Once they know about the problem, your current provider has the power to activate a cancel facility when slamming has occurred. If you can't resolve the problem or need further help, contact Otelo (Office of the Telecommunications Ombudsman, www.otelo.org.uk) which can investigate complaints.

If you don't act until after the ten-day period has passed, you may find you're already transferred to the new provider, which means your 'old' one now has limited powers to intervene. If this is the case, contact the 'new' provider explaining the problem. If you find you're now being billed by the 'new' company, contact Otelo, which has the power to intervene and investigate on your behalf. If you have been billed by a 'new' supplier and their charges exceed those of your previous one, Otelo has the power to sanction refunds.

Protect yourself

Most companies attempting slamming tactics actually initiate a call to you at some point, whether in person or via an automated system. So unless you've asked a new supplier to contact you, what's the best way to handle it? Simply hang up! Going ex-directory and ensuring you register with the Telephone Preference Service (0845 070 0707) can minimise your chances of being targeted, too, as it will drastically reduce the number of cold calls you receive.

Fake goods

This isn't about buying from someone with a suitcase in a back alley: fake goods are sold all over the world, so be on your guard when buying from market stalls, private sellers or discovering any 'too good to be true' prices.

The most common fake items include designer clothes, watches, perfumes, cosmetics, alcohol, CDs, DVDs, video games and computer software.

As well as being of poor quality in some cases, the knock-offs can be dangerous, like perfumes with a high alcohol content that can burn your skin, or dodgy alcohol that's little more than neat meths. Watch out for spelling mistakes on brand-name products or packaging that looks slightly different.

Foreign money scams

This one goes under various guises, but often it's a letter from someone abroad asking for your help to transfer money to the UK. There's usually a serious sob story involved, with many of these letters coming from Africa.

This one plays on your greed. By agreeing to the fraudster paying the money into your bank account, you'll be promised a big fat commission, but you'll have to divulge your bank account details first and, yes, you've guessed it, your account will be raided the second the fraudsters have your details.

Pass any of these letters to your local Trading Standards Office, or 'spam' the emails.

Phishing

Pronounced 'fishing', these emails pop into your inbox looking like they're from your bank. Usually the message asks you to validate your personal details by following a link that directs you to a 'fake' bank website. Once you've entered your personal details, the con artists are well on their way to raiding your account.

Contact the genuine version of the company yourself independently – for example, if you're suspicious of an email claiming to be from your bank, call your bank and ask them about it. Recently there have been cases of consumers getting suspicious emails that appear to be from the tax office saying they're due a rebate. Naturally they ask you to click on the link so you can give them details of your bank account to pay in the money.

Never reply to any emails like this or click on links within them. Many banks put warnings about bogus 'phishing' companies on their websites, so it is well worth reading these next time you log on so you know what to look out for.

Part

2

What to do when things go wrong

Things do go wrong; sadly it's a fact of life. It would be pretty amazing if none of us ever had a problem with anything we bought or paid for.

But when things go wrong, it's how you handle the situation that's most important. Knowing what to do and how to approach the problem can make the difference between feeling powerless and ripped off, or coming away a happy consumer.

When I presented a consumer phone-in programme a few years ago I was contacting companies every day, investigating customers' complaints. What was always interesting (and made great radio!) was the strange way some customers chose to tackle companies when things went wrong. In some cases they ended up totally alienating the company they claimed was at fault, simply by getting stroppy or rude; the end result being that a problem that could have been solved quickly and easily dragged on as the company then felt loathe to help.

In a classic case of 'two sides to a story', I remember one lady calling up complaining that her new computer had stopped working and the shop wouldn't repair it, despite the fact it was still under warranty. It all seemed a bit strange until we rang the shop. Funnily enough, their story was totally different. They told the tale of an angry and irate customer who'd marched in and threatened to throw her computer through their front window because it didn't work!

While we've all experienced some level of frustration when things go wrong, particularly if it's going to be time consuming to sort it out, or will mean a morning spent on the phone, it's always worth trying to keep your cool to get the job done quicker and get the result you want.

So this next section is about knowing your rights, arming yourself with the knowledge to confront companies if things go wrong, and how and what to do if they really won't budge.

Know your rights

As a savvy consumer it pays to know your rights, so if things go wrong (and they will do at some stage!), what started out as a great deal doesn't necessarily have to turn into a bad one.

This means knowing what your rights are and where you stand with faulty goods, buying online, returning unwanted gifts and cancelling contracts. In many cases we *think* we know our rights, but we often get it wrong, which means we don't get the result we want. And because we've *insisted* we're right, what starts out as a small problem escalates to a full-blown row in the middle of a busy store. So here's how to get it right *every* time.

High-street shopping

Shopping in the high street means you can 'try before you buy', but once you've taken that purchase home you've got fewer rights if you change your mind than you have buying online.

Know your rights (and you're on firmer ground!)

Know your rights *before you buy*. Don't rely on the knowledge of store sales staff, as sometimes they get things wrong. They may not be trained in consumer legislation and could mislead you simply because they don't know the rules.

By making sure you know *where* you stand *before* you buy, you'll feel more confident standing your ground if a problem occurs.

What the law says: the Sale of Goods Act

This is the bit of consumer law that lays down what you're entitled to when it comes to returning goods. The Sale of Goods Act says you can only return items that are *faulty*, not just because you've changed your mind. It says what you buy must be:

- *Fit for purpose* – this means it should do the job it's supposed to. If you buy a new TV and it doesn't work, it's not 'fit for purpose'.

- *As described* – if you buy a new tent for your camping holiday that's advertised as 'waterproof', yet on the first wet night the rain pours through, the item is faulty as it is not 'as described'.

- *Of satisfactory* – quality what you buy should be of decent quality and not fall to bits within five minutes. Although, depending on what you're buying and how much you're spending, some things will naturally last longer than others.

Faulty goods: refunds, repairs and exchanges

If what you've bought isn't fit for purpose, as described or of satisfactory quality, you can return it to the shop that sold it to you for a refund, repair or exchange.

But which of these options you get first is down to the retailer. In practice it's easier for large companies to offer refunds or exchange faulty goods, simply because of the time and cost involved in sending them away for repair. However, if you buy from smaller independent stores you may find they'll prefer to repair the item if they can, rather than hand over a refund from the till.

Tales from the shop floor

'Customers constantly get it wrong; they think if they buy something they can bring it back just because they change their mind.'

This was what one retail manager with over twenty years' experience told me. He says because so many of the big high-street names do go beyond their legal obligation and hand back refunds on unwanted items, customers *expect* everyone else to do the same. 'What customers don't realise is that coming in shouting about their rights (particularly when they get it wrong) doesn't make anyone want to help them out. If someone's honest and upfront we sometimes do bend the rules to try to help them out, but as it's down to our goodwill, a lot depends on their attitude.'

Refunds

If the store agrees the item's faulty and you've got proof of purchase it may offer you a refund. If you paid in cash you'll get cash back, and if you paid by card they'll put the refund back on the original card. So if you're returning something bought on your partner's card, you may have to settle for gift vouchers or a replacement unless the cardholder is with you.

Repairs

Under consumer law you've got to allow the seller a *reasonable* amount of time to repair the item, if that's the option they choose.

Retailers tend to favour the repair option with large purchases (typically dishwashers, washing machines or ovens) that aren't practical to bring back to the store. There are no time limits laid down in law as to how long they've got to fix it, but if you've had, say, five repairs within six months on the same washing machine, that wouldn't be considered reasonable and you can then ask for a replacement or refund.

Who's got the right to take back the goods?

Technically it's only the person who originally *bought* the item who's entitled to return it for a refund, repair or replacement, as it was they who entered into a 'contract' with the store; in other words, money and goods changed hands.

However, if you've been given an item as a gift, which turns out to be faulty, many stores will usually give you a refund or replace the broken item, providing you have a receipt or proof the item was recently purchased – in other words, you've not had it for ten years before bringing it back!

How long have I got to take it back?

Returning faulty goods within the first six months is usually straightforward, providing you've some form of proof of purchase. But beyond six months it's down to you to prove the item was faulty when you bought it. Naturally this can be hard to prove and in some cases, particularly with big items like sofas and beds, it may mean you've got to pay out for an independent expert to examine the product if the company won't accept responsibility for the fault.

Legally you can go back to the retailer for a refund, repair or replacement on faulty goods at any time up to *six years* after purchase. This comes from the EU's Guarantees Directive 1999, which came into force among member states in 2002, and is now incorporated into the Sale of Goods Act. But this doesn't mean you can stick the broken item at the back of a cupboard for five years before heading back to the store. You should always return faulty goods as soon as possible.

So if a store tries to claim you've no rights because you're one day outside its one-year warranty, or you've no case because you didn't buy an extended warranty – they're in the wrong. And when we talk about faults, this can be a problem that was there from the start or a fault that developed after use, for example a washing machine that won't spin or a toy that stops working. You can expect the store to refund, repair or replace the item up to the six-year limit, providing it's reasonable for the item to have lasted that long, but, as mentioned earlier, it's also down to you to prove it's always been faulty.

In some cases, if you've had the item a considerable time, you may be offered a partial, rather than a full refund. This takes into account the 'use' you've had from the item. This may happen if, say, you're returning a car because of a fault but you've had it nine months. The garage or dealership may decide to deduct an amount for 'wear and tear', as you've had the use of the car during this time.

A savvy consumer's story

Just because you're outside the store's 'guarantee' doesn't mean you've got no rights, as this story shows.

'We bought a washing machine from a high-street store. As it was a top-of-the-range machine we expected it to last a few years, but just thirteen months later it broke down. It was outside the store's one-year warranty so we called out a local repair engineer, who said the thermostat was at fault and it would cost £80 to repair. We needed a working machine so we had to pay up. Feeling unhappy, as we'd been advised in the store that these machines were "built to last", we wrote to the manufacturer's head office and told them what had happened. Less than a week later they wrote back, enclosing a cheque for the full cost of the repair.

It turned me back into a happy consumer – and all for the price of a stamp!'

Proof of purchase

Lots of us get confused over this – what counts as proof of purchase? You don't actually need the receipt in order to get a refund, replacement or repair on faulty goods – it's having 'proof of purchase' that counts. This can be anything from the original till receipt to a credit card or bank statement showing when the item was bought.

If you're returning 'non-faulty' goods to a store that offers goodwill refunds, they *may* insist on the original till receipt before they'll pay out. Without this, you can often still get an exchange or store gift vouchers, providing you can prove the item was bought in the store – if, for example, there's an obvious store label or stamp on the product. But the amount you'll be given will usually be the 'last selling price', so if the item's now half price in the sale, that's the price you'll get. You won't get full price without being able to prove that's what you paid.

It is worth keeping receipts for at least six months for smaller items and up to six years with large items. Put them in a notebook and keep a folder for guarantees and instructions. And hang on to the box or packaging for at least a month, until you know the product works. That's not to say you can't return it after that time; of course you can, but if the item breaks after a week it looks better to be able to take it back to the store in its original packaging.

Don't fall for the 'fob off' (or how to stand your ground!)

'You'll need to contact the manufacturer.' This is a classic cop out. You return with faulty goods and the store tells you it's not their problem and you must contact the manufacturer, giving you the runaround. Where do you stand?

Your 'contract' is with the store (that's a 'contract' in the sense that money and goods changed hands on their premises, therefore a deal was done), so it's the *store* that must take responsibility for sorting out the problem. If they won't co-operate, contact their head office.

Sue's savvy stories – it happened to me

I should say first up that I'm always very good about keeping receipts, though clearly not on this occasion. I bought a non-stick wok from a high-street store and paid by credit card. By the third time I'd used it, the 'non-stick' part had worn off so, after hunting around for the receipt, I decided to use my credit card bill as my proof of purchase.

This listed the full amount of the transaction (as I'd also bought some other things in store) along with the date and name of store. So I rang them up, explained the problem and they were able to search their system to find an itemised list of what I'd bought that day, including the faulty wok.

So I popped in and got a full refund back on my card.

Faulty goods checklist

- Don't dither – always return goods as soon as possible.
- Take the item to the store you bought it from; or, if it's a large chain, another branch will do.
- Make sure you've got some form of proof of purchase.
- Don't waste time queuing at the till, head straight for the customer service or refund counter.
- Be polite but assertive. Outline the problem and say whether it's a refund, exchange or repair you'd like.
- If you're not happy with what's being offered, ask to see a more senior member of staff.
- If you need further advice, contact your local Citizens Advice (you'll find the number in your local phone book) or Consumer Direct: www.consumerdirect.gov.uk or 08454 04 05 06.

What happens if I change my mind or it's an unwanted gift?

Too big, too small, the wrong colour or an unwanted gift; you can usually get a refund in most high-street stores, as they have generous returns policies which go far beyond what's expected by law. They'll often refund you in cash or back on the card that was used for the purchase, providing you've got the receipt, or on a store gift card if not.

But they don't *have* to; this is a goodwill gesture on their part which, being so big, they can afford to do; but smaller outlets can't usually match this, so always make sure you check a store's refund policy *before* you buy. Don't just assume they'll swap or refund you simply because most of the other high-street stores do.

Some items, like food and cosmetics, are exempt from refunds (unless damaged or faulty) due to hygiene reasons. If, however, you've bought the item online, by phone or mail order, the rules are different, as you haven't had the chance to see the goods before buying, so you have at least seven *working* days from the date of delivery to return the item for a refund. (There's more on this later in the chapter.)

High-street refunds

Here's what some of the big high-street names offer on unwanted purchases:

- *Marks & Spencer* – 35 days for a refund with receipt; without one you'll get an exchange or credit vouchers to the last selling price.
- *Argos* – 30-day money-back guarantee, providing the item is unused, in its original packaging and with the receipt.
- *John Lewis* – 28 days for a refund with receipt, providing the item is in its original undamaged packaging.
- *Next* – 28 days for a refund with receipt; without one you'll get an exchange or refund at the last selling price on a gift card.

Refunds on sale items

In this situation you've got the same rights as you have when paying full price. That means refunds, repairs or replacements for faulty or damaged goods, providing you've got proof of purchase. Most larger stores will offer goodwill refunds on unwanted sale items, providing you've got the receipt.

The law is strict on sale items and stores can only class items as 'sale' goods if they've genuinely been sold previously at a higher price. This stops stores shipping in a load of rubbish and making you think you've got a bargain because you bought it in the 'sale'.

Forget extended warranties

Flogging extended warranties is big business for the high-street stores and rakes in huge profits; but remember some stores offer free two-year warranties on electrical items anyway. And, as mentioned earlier, under EU consumer legislation you can return faulty items any time up to six years (providing it's reasonable for them to last this long and you've got some form of proof of purchase), so don't be fobbed off just because you didn't buy an extended warranty.

A big problem with extended warranties is that you're restricted to who can repair the item if it develops a fault; you've got to call the warranty company first and in some cases you may find you're waiting a week for someone to look at, say, your washing machine, whereas you could get it repaired yourself in a much shorter time. There's also often a whole list of exclusions as to what's not covered, so, in my opinion, they're just not worth the paper they're written on.

If you do buy an extended warranty in store and then change your mind, providing the warranty lasts for a year or more you've got forty-five days in which to cancel. This comes under the Extended Warranties on Domestic Electrical Goods Order 2005 Fair Trading Act. If you want to cancel, look for the contact address on the paperwork you've been given and write to them saying that this is what you want to do, and ask for written confirmation that this has been done.

Protect yourself with your credit card

This could sound like a boring old bit of jargon, *but* Section 75 of the 1974 Consumer Credit Act is actually a great bit of legislation that gives you added protection when paying by credit card. If you're buying something that costs between £100 and £30,000 and you pay even the smallest part of it with your credit card, you're automatically protected in the event the goods don't turn up, the company goes bust or the goods are faulty.

Under the 1974 Consumer Credit Act you can go back to your credit card company for a refund, as Section 75 makes both the supplier of the goods and your credit card company jointly liable. Always go back to the company you paid your money to first, but if they won't play ball or help out, contact your credit card company.

And the good news is that this applies whenever you use your card anywhere in the world – whether online, by phone or in person – providing what you're buying cost between £100 and £30,000.

But this protection only applies to credit cards, not payment by charge cards, store cards, debit cards, cash or cheques. Visa, however, does operate a scheme for debit card customers where you can claim a refund in the event of problems (there's more on this in Chapter 7).

Shopping online, by phone or mail order

Sometimes you can't get to the high street, or it's simply more convenient to order items from the comfort of your armchair. Nowadays there are many more options, such as buying from a TV shopping channel, ordering from a catalogue, or shopping online.

The Distance Selling Regulations

In the EU when you shop online, by phone, TV shopping channel or mail order, you have more rights than in the high street. All the usual ones apply – so items must be *fit for purpose, as described* and *of satisfactory quality* – but because you won't have had the chance to examine the goods prior to buying them, as you would in the high street, you are given an extra cooling-off period to give you time to change your mind and get a refund.

This is thanks to the Distance Selling Regulations, which state that you have seven working days to return your item (starting the day after you receive the goods).

Financial products *aren't* covered under the Distance Selling Regulations, so if you're buying insurance or taking out a new credit card you've got different rights. (There's more on this in Chapter 7 about banks and financial services.)

> **When buying online**
>
> ● Always make a note of the company's details. This should include the address and phone number – including a landline number, not just a mobile.
>
> ● Check delivery charges or shipping costs and VAT before buying. If you're buying from overseas you may be liable for customs duty in the UK, depending on the value of the item.
>
> ● Once you've ordered, print a copy of your confirmation, along with any order numbers.

Website safety and security

● An online shopping web address should always start with https:// – the 's' stands for secure.

● Look for the small padlock icon at the bottom of the screen; this shows the site is encrypted so your details will be scrambled when you enter your card details for payment.

● Keep anti-virus software up to date and use your firewall protection to keep your computer security at a maximum.

Where are they trading?

If the company you're buying from is based outside the EU, you won't be covered under EU consumer law for faulty goods. If you're buying online from a trader outside the EU, it's worth paying by credit card (providing the full cost of the item is between £100 and £30,000) so that you can go back to your credit card company for a refund if the goods are faulty, don't turn up, or the company you buy from goes bust.

> ## Consumer legislation – the bite sized chunks to remember
>
> ### Sale of Goods Act
>
> This gives you the right to a refund, exchange or repair if the item's faulty, not as described or not fit for the purpose.
>
> ### Vouchers or cash?
>
> If the item's faulty, you don't have to accept vouchers or credit notes: you can insist on a refund, repair or replacement, providing you've got proof of purchase. If you've had the item for some time the store will usually offer to repair it in the first instance, but if it can't be fixed within a reasonable time you should get a refund.
>
> ### Online sales
>
> The Distance Selling Regulations cover items bought by phone, mail order or online. You've got seven *working* days to return items if you change your mind, as you can't examine them before buying.

Cancelling contracts

Signed up to buy double glazing and changed your mind, or decided against that new bathroom suite? You can cancel, but depending on *where* you are when you signed on the dotted line your rights are different.

Buying at home

You've got seven days to cancel most contracts made in your home. It makes no difference whether you asked the company to call or whether they 'cold-called' – that's turning up unannounced on your doorstep. There are exceptions to this; if what you're buying costs under £35, or if you're buying perishable goods like flowers or food products, or land or insurance. These rules come under the Cancellation of Contracts made in a Consumer's Home or Place of Work etc. Regulations 2008.

Buying at a trader's premises

You've got pretty much zero rights, unless of course what you're buying turns out to be faulty.

Buying services by phone or online

You've got seven days to cancel and the seven days start the day *after* you agreed to the service. This is under the Distance Selling Regulations. If, however, you agreed that the service would start immediately, you automatically lose your right to the cooling-off period.

The regulations don't cover financial services, holiday or travel arrangements, made-to-measure items, or perishable goods (including food or CDs and DVDs)

Buying privately

Buy privately and you've got less rights than buying from a recognised trader.

The rules about fit for purpose and of satisfactory quality go out of the window with private sellers, as these only apply to businesses. But with private sellers goods must still be as described. If not, you may have a case to ask for your money back.

Some traders try to pretend they're private individuals for the purpose of selling items, as this means buyers have less rights. Watch out for this, for example when buying cars through the small ads.

Some sellers on internet auction sites are traders and have their own shop window online, which means you've got more rights. But just like buying from a car boot sale, if you buy privately from an individual it's very much a case of 'buyer beware', so check out what you're buying first.

If you're buying online through eBay, you've added protection if you pay by PayPal, which is eBay's approved payment system. (There's more about this in Chapter 11 on buying and selling on eBay.)

And if you're advertising in the small ads be wary of how much personal information you give in your advert. You don't have to list a phone number; if you prefer, just give an email address or you can use options like Autotrader's 'Telesafe', which automatically vets callers and blocks any calls from traders who've been previously blacklisted (and also stops nuisance calls).

How to complain and get what you want

Sometimes things do go wrong. It's a fact of life, and it's important to know how to handle these situations so that you come away with the best possible outcome. Yet many of us are afraid of speaking up and complaining; we feel nervous and are more likely to nod when asked if everything's OK in a restaurant rather than tell them the food's cold or the service slow.

But complaining doesn't make you a stroppy consumer, and saying something if you're not happy is essential when it comes to getting value for money. Always remember, you've paid with your hard-earned cash, so why shouldn't you get what you've paid for?

That said, there's a real art to complaining effectively. We've probably all heard loud complainers who think they'll get what they want by drawing attention to themselves, yet a complaint made in a friendly, short and succinct way often gets a quicker result – and usually the one you want.

So, here's how to get your point across and get results.

Don't be afraid to complain

Head Stateside and you won't catch the Americans settling for poor service, so why should we? Would you throw £20 down the nearest drain? No? Well, why waste that or even more, simply because it feels a bit awkward to complain?

Yes, complaining can be daunting and intimidating at times, but if you don't speak up you may go away an unhappy customer, feeling you've been ripped off or had a poor deal. It's so much better to know what to do and say, so that you can handle the situation effectively and get what you deserve.

Complaining in the right way will get results, but it's knowing *how* to complain, who to speak to and what to say that can speed up the process, avoiding much of the frustration and time wasting that can often be as annoying as the initial problem.

Don't go mad

The worst mistake you can make (apart from not bothering to complain) is to shout or scream at the first person you speak to. They may not be in a position of authority and if you do this in shops it could mean you're asked to leave or risk security being called. While it's frustrating and annoying if you've had poor service or shoddy goods, you won't get anywhere by letting rip at the first person you see or speak to.

You'll actually get better results by staying calm and confident.

How to complain *effectively*

We all make mistakes – nobody's perfect – but what sets the good companies apart from the poor ones is how they handle those mistakes. Do they try to cover up any problems or make excuses? Or do they hold their hands up, apologise and try to fix things?

Sorting out the problem could mean anything from a discounted bill to the offer of a free bottle of wine in a restaurant, or a goodwill payment or gift voucher from a company that's messed up.

While some companies will immediately *offer* to put things right, with others you'll have to ask and say what you want. Say you've had a disappointing meal in a restaurant; in some cases if the company can get away with just an apology, they will. This is why, just like when you're negotiating on price, you need to say what you want.

So, using the restaurant scenario, if you're complaining that your meal is cold and it's going to take twenty minutes to cook a replacement, it's reasonable to expect complementary drinks while you wait, or you may prefer a reduction on the bill?

Tactics for complaining in person, by phone or letter

Complaining isn't fun, nobody enjoys doing it, but if you don't do something when things go wrong, you run the risk of being ripped off.

Complaining in person

Whatever the problem is, complain quickly and give the company the chance to put things right as soon as possible. Don't leave without a word and then write a stroppy letter to head office a week later.

In shops, if you've got faulty goods (as explained in the last chapter) you should go back to the store as soon as possible, along with a proof of purchase. If the problem can't be solved there or you want to speak to someone more senior, ask for the store manager. If you still can't get the result you want, that is the time to contact the company's head office.

In restaurants, always speak to the person serving you *before* asking for the manager, as in any decent restaurant it's the waiting staff who should check you're happy with your meal. They may be able to fix the problem; if not, ask for the manager.

And with hotels, cinemas, airlines, garages, hairdressers or any other service providers, speak to the person who did the job; if it can't be resolved, go a step higher, asking for the most senior person.

If you're nervous, get someone to come with you for moral support; but agree who's going to do the talking so you're not *both* trying to complain at the same time, which can come across as being aggressive.

Complaining by phone

If it's not practical to complain face to face, say you're dealing with a company based in the other end of the country, ring them as soon as possible. Speak to the person who handled your booking, order or contract first. Tell them why you're not happy and what you'd like to be done.

If they can't resolve the situation, ask to speak to a more senior member of staff. If you're ringing a call centre because of a problem with a supplier, say a gas, electricity or phone company, and can't get the result you want, ask for the disconnections department. These people are responsible for trying to hang on to customers and they can usually pull out all the stops to fix the problem and authorise refunds or compensation. I've often done this, particularly when I can't get problems resolved with my mobile phone company, and it's amazing how quickly things turn around when you get this far.

Phone complaint checklist

- Jot down what the problem is and what you want; this will help if you get nervous.

- Keep receipts, paperwork, booking numbers and order forms to hand.

- Make a note of the name and number of the person you speak to; the date and time is also useful, as many companies record calls so the conversation can be traced. I usually write this on the original paperwork so details are kept together.

- Call-centre staff are notoriously hard to pin down with names; they'll often only give out their first name, so ask for their department and which call centre they're in. Get a job number and ask for details of your conversation to be logged on your account.

Complaining by letter or email

Always go to the top. Write directly to the company's chief executive by name, not to an anonymous person within the company. Simply addressing your letter to a random person like 'Head of Customer Services' may mean your letter is passed around the entire company five times over if there's nobody with that actual title and everyone's 'passing the buck'.

If you don't know the name of the top person, call the company to find out or 'Google' them and make sure you get the spelling right. The reason for going to the top is that these people are *most* concerned with the company's reputation and good name and will usually nudge someone to fix the problem quickly.

Keep it personal

Think about the person reading your letter. Making it personal is a good trick as you're more likely to grab their attention. This way they'll actually read your letter, rather than giving it a quick cursory glance.

There was a truly brilliant one that did the rounds on the internet after it was sent to a top airline boss regarding the in-flight meals. While anyone reading your letter won't want your life history, if you can connect with them (or make them laugh), your complaint is more likely to stick in their mind and they'll want to do something about it. This works especially well with small retailers who won't (hopefully) have the volume of complaints that a larger national organisation might, so they probably take the time to read each letter individually.

I can still remember consumer cases from radio shows I presented a few years ago, simply because of the stories involved. The ones who ranted and raved have long since been forgotten, but the more entertaining people or those with a story to tell have always stuck in my mind.

Keep your letter or email short, succinct and to the point. Reams of paperwork stapled together or email attachments are guaranteed to put someone off reading them properly. Make sure you include any reference or booking numbers in your letter and if you need to attach copies of relevant paperwork, do so, but make sure they're only *copies*.

Finally, check you've got the company's correct address and always include your own contact details; if you prefer to be contacted by email, say so and include the address, or if you're out at work give your work or mobile number. Send your letter Recorded Signed For; which means it requires a signature at the other end so you have proof that it's arrived.

Sue's savvy stories – it happened to me

This is the story of a girlie lunch that wasn't up to scratch, but rather than trying to fob us off, the pub in question pulled out all the stops to turn us back into happy customers.

I went for lunch with my friend Peggy at a gorgeous country pub that we'd been to before and always had fabulous food. Peggy ordered a smoked salmon and cream cheese sandwich, which arrived complete with a large sliver of plastic from the soft cheese tub. Now we could have said nothing and grumbled and groaned our way through lunch vowing never to go there again, but we didn't. I called over the lady who'd brought out our food and explained the problem. She looked absolutely mortified, apologised profusely and said she'd sort it out immediately.

Minutes later she was back and replaced Peggy's lunch, didn't charge us for either of the lunches and offered us coffee and desserts on the house! Now while we didn't complain to get the 'freebies', her attitude was clearly a great one about keeping customers happy and we've both been back on many occasions since.

How to complain and get results

- Be pleasant and friendly. It sounds obvious, but get people on your side and they'll *want* to help.

- With faulty goods, check your rights first so that you know where you stand if things get tricky. Keep a note of conversations, dates and times to back up your case.

- Keep evidence like receipts, tags or labels to prove where items were bought if you're returning faulty goods.

- If you're writing a letter, make it clear and concise; a lengthy five-page saga is unlikely to be read properly.

- Say what you want: money off, a replacement or compensation for your inconvenience.

- Go to the top. Ask for or write to the most senior person in the company; they'll be most concerned about the company image and often have the power to make instant decisions.

- Don't feel you have to accept their first offer; remember the 'haggling' game? Negotiating for a mutually acceptable outcome to a problem is just the same. If the company is offering to replace your dining room suite but can't come for over a week, tell them it's not good enough and try to negotiate a more immediate date.

I can't get a result – what next?

If despite writing, phoning and even going to the top you feel you're getting nowhere, you've still got a couple of options. Speak to Consumer Direct (08454 04 05 06) or your local Citizens Advice for further advice on how to proceed in your specific situation. They can, in some cases, refer the matter to Trading Standards, who can contact the company on your behalf.

Find out if the company you're dealing with is a member of a trade organisation. They usually have a code of conduct for member companies and will investigate complaints from customers.

Beyond that, find out if there is an ombudsman service for final adjudication. In many cases you'll have to go through the appropriate channels of complaint first; in other words you can't short circuit the system and go direct to the ombudsman – you'll usually need to show that you've written directly to the company and any trade organisation first.

Small Claims Court

This is the last resort. If you've exhausted all other channels of complaint and you're not able to reach an amicable solution, you can take your case to the county court, or Small Claims Court as it tends to be known.

Don't apply to the county court *before* you've given the company concerned the chance to put things right, as you could be penalised by the court. This may mean paying the other party's expenses and costs in attending court if you've asked for the case to be held prematurely.

How the Small Claims Court works

- It's set up to be quick, cheap and unintimidating; a user-friendly style of court.
- You can represent yourself so there's no need for expensive solicitors.
- It's meant for claims of £5,000 or less, although with personal injury claims the limit is lower – at £1,000.

Before taking your case to the Small Claims Court it's worth getting legal advice. A cost-effective way to do this is by getting a list of local solicitors who offer a fixed-fee advice service from your local Citizens Advice. This will typically cost around £20 for twenty to thirty minutes' advice. You won't be short-changed on advice; this isn't a watered down version of what they'd tell the full-fee paying customers, but a great way to get some legal advice if it's a one-off issue you need to ask about.

Before you issue a claim

It is worth a quick game of bluff before you officially lodge your complaint, as this can often bring results and avoid the court process.

Contact your local county court for the paperwork (this won't cost you a penny, as it's lodging the claim that incurs a fee), fill them in and date them a week in advance. Then send a copy to the person you're in dispute with, along with a covering letter, telling them that on this date you'll be lodging the complaint with your local county court.

It's a ruse I've suggested to people on consumer programmes and in several cases it's worked, as the company concerned then realise (if they know they're in the wrong) that they're likely to come off worst if the case goes to court. So they usually pay up.

Before you make a claim consider whether the person you're suing has the means to pay you if you're successful. If they're on the verge of bankruptcy, even if you win the case you may have to wait some considerable time (or forever) for your money.

A savvy consumer's story

While the idea of going to 'court' can be daunting, taking a case to the Small Claims Court can mean the difference between getting your money back or losing out, as this case from a successful claimant shows.

'I'd asked a building company to repoint the side of my house. I paid a deposit but one day into the job they'd made a mess of it and walked off.

They'd got my deposit but wouldn't come back to finish the job, and were quite nasty on the phone, threatening to sue me for the remainder of the money they said I owed them.

I spoke to my local Citizens Advice who suggested getting an independent surveyor to look at the work. He gave me a report saying it wasn't done properly, so I filled in the paperwork to take my case to the Small Claims Court. It was very straightforward and a friend helped me. Just a week before the case was due in court, the building company settled 'out of court', giving me back my deposit and court fees.'

Making a claim

- Get a claim form from your local county court or download one at www.hmcourts-service.gov.uk.

- As the claimant, you can apply to have the case heard in your local county court, although it may be held in the defendant's local county court, so be aware of where they're based.

- Complete two copies of the form and return both to the court along with the fee. Make sure you keep a copy for your own records too.

How much does it cost?

Fees are based on a sliding scale; for claims up to £3,000 there's an £85 fee which you must send to your local county court with your completed forms. For claims over £3,000 and up to the £5,000 limit, it's £108. In some cases if you're claiming benefits you may not have to pay.

Part

3

Getting the best deal in practice

So, you now know the principles of getting the best deal and what to do when things go wrong, but while knowing the theory is all good grounding, you need to know how to put it into practice.

It's a bit like having an instruction manual; you read it and think you know everything, but there'll always be something unexpected that happens to throw you.

So while it's not possible to cover every potential scenario, the next few chapters will cover the main situations you're likely to come up against in your search for the best deal and getting value for money.

They will give you lots of ideas for getting the best for less, including sneaky ways to save on your bills; get the most competitive deals and rates on mortgages; and how to get the best deal on your holiday, including tips on when to fly for the cheapest deals and how to save money on car hire. They will also give you advice on what to do if you get into debt and how to extricate yourself.

And of course getting the best deal can be about *making* some extra cash too. I mentioned earlier in the book about selling on items you no longer need, so there's a whole chapter on eBay and how to buy and sell, along with tips on how to boost your final selling price or find the bargains that others miss. Currently three million of us make at least £10 a week using eBay, but when it comes to your rights, how many of us know what to do if something we buy arrives broken or turns out to be faulty? Do we just put it down to bad luck or can we in fact get our money back?

And there's my guide to spotting the cowboys and how to avoid being ripped off when you come across one of those 'too good to be true' deals – and how to make sure your hard-earned cash stays in your own pocket rather than someone else's.

Utility companies

Because you're not able to negotiate face to face, getting the best deal on household bills can seem more daunting than shopping around for the best deal on the high street.

And there's no two ways about it, shopping around for your gas and electricity doesn't really excite anyone. *But* it is worth doing, as you can save some serious cash. And when you've got the best deal on those, you can carry on and get the best deal on your phone, your broadband and TV package …

This chapter tells you in practical terms what to look for, what to ask for and how to avoid paying a fortune.

Energy bills

If you want to reduce your everyday costs for heating, lighting and power, you need to negotiate cheaper gas and electricity bills.

Too lazy to switch supplier?

If you're on a bog-standard deal and just pay up when the bill arrives, you may as well throw a chunk of your hard-earned cash down the nearest drain.

Switching suppliers to get a better deal is really easy. There's no pipework to change; it's just a case of another company billing you for your gas or electricity, or both if you opt for a 'dual fuel' deal.

And even if you're feeling smug because you've switched suppliers once, if you haven't shopped around within the last year you can probably still save money by switching again. As with any deal, the best one right now may not still be the best in six months' or a year's time, as prices and terms and conditions change.

According to the energy regulator Ofgem, households switching both gas and electricity *can* cut bills by over £100 a year, and some of the price comparison websites claim it's a lot more – up to £300 a year. So, where do you start?

Finding the best deal

Sit down with a cup of coffee and your previous year's energy bills and work out how much gas and electricity you've used and what you've paid for it. If you can't find your bills or have thrown them away, take your current meter readings and call your suppliers for the previous year's readings. This way you can work out exactly how much energy you've used and what you've paid for it.

The next step is easy: use one of the many online comparison sites like www.uswitch.com or www.moneysupermarket.com to find a better deal for you. All you have to do is put in your address, size of property and cost of bills and it comes up with cheaper options. Then call those companies directly to check the prices are right and that you're eligible for the deal. Don't just use one comparison site, try a couple of different ones.

Switching supplies through some comparison sites may mean you're eligible for a cash-back payment too. But remember, the savings will only be as good as the information you give, so if you're second guessing what you currently use, the savings could look bigger.

You can also cut the cost still further by switching to online billing rather then paper bills, and paying by direct debit to qualify for a discount.

Try to avoid doing a price comparison in the aftermath of any big price rises, as this may skew any savings you're looking at if other companies are still in the process of putting their prices up (or down).

If you decide to switch, you can do the paperwork online and your new supplier will take care of the time-consuming stuff like telling your old supplier you're leaving, doing the meter readings and getting the final bill sent out.

If you've found a better deal, it's always worth a call to your existing supplier to see if they can price-match. Ask for the disconnections department or press the option that says, 'if you're thinking of leaving us', and then ask if they can give you a discount or move you to a better deal.

Top tips to get a better deal (and save money)

- Swap paper for online bills to get a discount.

- Don't pay by cheque or cash – switch to direct debit. It's quick and easy for suppliers so you'll get a discount for prompt payment and never face another red bill again.

- Do your own readings. If you get an estimated bill, check the meter yourself. If you've used less than the estimated figure, call the company (or with online billing enter the reading yourself) to get the bill updated so you're not paying more than you should. This works in reverse too, as there's nothing worse than receiving a massive bill in six months' time if the energy company has wildly *under*-estimated your usage.

- Dual fuel deals (buying both gas and electricity from the same supplier) *can* often be cheaper, but not always.

- Don't use a pre-payment meter unless you absolutely have to. This is often the case if you're living in rented accommodation, but you'll pay far more for your energy this way.

- Review your deal every year. Prices go up and down, so the best deal right now may not be the best in a year's time.

- There are lots of smaller ways to cut the cost of your bills, including turning down the heating thermostat by one degree, using a thirty-degree wash, switching off lights when you leave the room and not leaving your appliances on standby.

Are you properly insulated?

Saving money switching energy suppliers is all well and good, but if your home is poorly insulated you're paying for heat you don't use, so make your home more energy efficient.

- Get double glazing installed, or replaced if you've got old frames. The average householder wastes £140 a year by losing heat through draughty windows and doors.
- Insulate your loft. This can save over £200 a year in energy bills. You can buy rolls of the stuff from most DIY stores, and around 250mm thick is the recommended depth.
- Lag your hot water tank. Buy it a warm jacket (British standard ones are at least 75mm thick) and you can knock £40 a year off your bills.

Are you eligible for any grants?

Depending on your household income you can get up to £2,700 in Government grants to boost your home's energy efficiency. This includes installing central heating, loft insulation and draught proofing. Across England the scheme's called 'Warm Front', and those over sixty and on certain benefits are eligible, as are those with children (under sixteen) who claim benefits such as income support and council tax benefit.

Once your application has been approved, an assessor visits your property and helps you prioritise which energy-saving measures are needed. They can then arrange for approved companies to do the work for you free of charge. For more information go to www.warmfront.co.uk.

Energy suppliers for new-build properties

Just because the developer negotiates the initial contract to get you hooked up doesn't mean you've got to stay with the same energy supplier. It's important to find out which supplier you're with as quickly as possible, too, as they may not be the cheapest. The energy regulator Ofgem says it's the developers' responsibility to sort out the initial energy contracts, but the developers are unlikely to shop around on price; usually just going for the big-name companies or the prominent supplier in the area.

Finding your suppliers

If you've bought a new build and are unsure of your energy suppliers, here's what to do:

- Contact your builder or site sales office. Check you've got both your 'plot' number and 'door' number, as these get confused by both consumers and energy companies.

- If the builder can't tell you, look on your meters for the serial numbers – usually eight or nine digits long. These can then be used to trace the supplier.

- To find your electricity supplier, call your local distribution company and ask for their Meter Point Administration Service (MPAS), giving them your address and code number from your meter. You can find contact numbers for the local distribution companies from Consumer Direct by calling 08454 04 05 06.

- To trace your gas supplier you'll need to contact the transporter, which for the majority of customers will be either National Grid, Northern Gas Networks, Scotland Gas Networks, Southern Gas Networks or Wales & West Utilities. You'll need to call a centralised number (0870 608 1524) to find out who your supplier is, but if they can't help you it may be that your supply is via an independent gas transporter (IGT). Once again, Consumer Direct should have a list of contact details for these across different areas of the country.

If you're finding it impossible to trace your energy suppliers, the good news for domestic customers is that they can only be 'back-billed' for a maximum of a year. This was previously six years, although the caveat attached means you must be able to show you've made reasonable attempts to trace your supplier, for example supplying letters as written proof.

Mobile phones

If you're on a contract deal and regularly go beyond your call and text allowance, you're not getting the best deal.

Once you exceed this allowance you'll usually be charged standard-rate prices; so it's much cheaper to negotiate a deal with more inclusive minutes and texts. If you rarely use up your minute and text bundle, consider switching to a cheaper (and lower-rate) deal as you're paying for a service you don't need or use.

We spend an average of £18 a month on our mobile package, yet over half of us don't look at what we're getting for our money when we choose a deal. We're more likely to be swayed by any 'free' gifts on offer, or the brand of handset, than actual value for money. A survey by the financial comparison website moneysupermarket.com says 20 per cent of us haven't negotiated a new contract for over a year; which means we're wasting money, as once our current deals end we should be trying to negotiate a better one.

Don't wait for your current contract to end. The best time to negotiate is a month before it's up for renewal. First work out what you want and need from your mobile phone package. Is it more or less minutes or texts for your money, a new phone, or the lot?

Check out what other deals are available, using the price comparison websites to help you, then call your supplier and ask what they can do for you in the way of a better deal. Your provider is *bound* to come up with an offer. If it's not enough or not the deal you want, push a bit more! What you do is say you're thinking of leaving and ask to be put through to the disconnections department. Or if you're feeling bold, bypass the first bit and just ask to speak to disconnections straight away. As I've said before, in the disconnections department it's their job to *keep* customers, so within reason they'll do whatever they can to keep you on the books. These are also the people to call if you've had a problem with your service and can't get it resolved; funny how quickly they'll turn an issue around once you get this far!

And remember that if you do decide to leave for a better deal with another supplier, you *can* still take your phone number with you. You'll need a PAC (Port Authorisation Code) from your current supplier – which is basically a reference number that you give to your new provider to transfer your number across. Watch out for some companies that may try to charge you for this or just drag their heels when it comes to handing it over.

Using your mobile abroad

The holiday blues may kick in the moment you're home, but it's more likely to be several weeks before you feel the financial impact – in the form of your mobile phone bill.

Taking a mobile on holiday is essential for most of us. Family will want to know you've arrived safely or you may need to make the occasional work call; and even *if* you check the call charges *before* heading off, chances are you could still be in for a nasty shock, with some calls costing as much as £2 per minute.

EU legislation has meant the cost of both making and receiving calls from abroad is coming down; currently it stands at 38p per minute to make calls and 19p per minute to receive them. But that's only within the EU.

Easy ways to cut your call costs include choosing which network to switch to abroad. Most phones automatically lock on to the strongest signal; this is when you get that 'hello and welcome' style text. Ask your provider if they're partnered with any foreign networks as it's relatively easy to change networks on your phone, usually by going into the 'settings' option.

Switching off your voicemail when abroad can save money. Even if your phone's off, you'll pay the bulk of the call cost from the UK when someone leaves a voicemail *and* you'll pay again to retrieve the message. Unless you need to check calls, ask your network provider to temporarily remove the voicemail facility.

Watch out for hefty data roaming charges if you use your phone to surf online while abroad. One case that hit the headlines was a holidaymaker who downloaded three TV shows to her mobile phone while abroad, costing her a hefty £5,000. As with call costs, check prices before you go, and if you think you'll lose track of time set an alarm for, say, five or ten minutes, so you know exactly how much time you've used.

Broadband and TV services

Paying different companies for your home phone, broadband and TV package means you're probably not getting the best deal.

Combining these into one package with one provider is usually the best way to save money, with a typical annual household saving of around £250.

But there can be downsides to what's known as 'bundling' – combining telecoms services with the same provider. The two big things to weigh up are the speed you need and whether you're prepared to have a download cap on your broadband. If you just like to check your emails during the evening or only use the net to search for holiday deals or online shopping, fast download speeds won't be top of your priority list, so don't be lured into signing up for super-speed deals. But if, say, you regularly download music and videos or work from home, fast download speeds and no caps will probably be a must-have.

But while the price on paper might look good, watch out for hidden charges like costs for late payment, paper billing and installation fees. Very often companies will waive any installation fee if you push for it, or if you're prepared to sign up for longer than the standard minimum-term contract.

When it comes to TV packages, watch for companies offering unlimited channels free for an introductory period. Most will want your bank details when you first join, and if you don't call them before the introductory offer ends to say which services you want in your regular package you can find you're paying for the lot, and you'll usually end up locked into a contract for a minimum term of around a year.

Check before signing up

- What's the cost if you exceed your download limit?
- What's the call centre cost if you need technical help? These can be expensive – at around £1 a minute.
- Are there any initial set-up or installation fees and charges?
- Is there a minimum contract term?
- Are there any penalties if you move home or want to switch provider?

Getting through to the right people (or how to find a cheaper number to dial)

Need help with your broadband service? Want to call your energy supplier about a problem on your bill? Easier said than done, as you'll often find you're calling an 0845, 0844 or 0870 number that won't be included in any 'free' minutes you get with your home or mobile phone package. *And* calling these numbers generates extra cash for the companies concerned, as they can get a cut of call costs!

0845 and 0870 numbers are often used by big companies like banks, hospitals and businesses. Known as 'non-geographic' numbers, you can't tell which area of the country you're calling.

- These numbers are often used for call centres, as it saves changing numbers if they move location.
- Ten minutes is the average wait time on these numbers, according to the Consumers' Association, which means you can quickly run up a hefty bill.
- Charges vary according to which phone you're calling from. Dialling 0870 from a landline can cost 10p a minute, and around 35p from mobiles. BT has recently abolished charges for dialling 0845 and 0870 numbers for customers signed up to its inclusive minute deals.

So, find a cheaper way to call:

- *Look for the 03 numbers* – calls to these numbers cost the same (or less) than the standard 01 and 02 prefixes and *are* included in any free-minute bundles.

- *Avoid 0870 numbers* – don't automatically dial the 0870 number that's given. If you're calling your bank or credit card company, look on the back of your statement for a 'calling from overseas' number. This is usually always a standard landline number, so if you knock off the 44 code (needed to dial the UK from abroad) this cuts the cost of your call. It may even be free if you've got inclusive minutes to landlines as part of your home or mobile deal.

- *Check out the www.saynoto0870.com website* – this lists alternative lower-cost landline and freephone numbers for lots of companies. Type in the company you want and it lists alternative numbers. Or use an online free directory enquiry service like www.bt.com to find standard landline numbers for a branch or head office of the company. Then ask to be put through to the relevant department.

- *Call in using the 'new customer' line* – I bet they'll answer the phone faster and you'll often find numbers for new customers are free or cheaper than the customer service number. Once you're connected, ask to be put through to the right department and this time you won't pay the 0870 charge when you're on hold!

Banks and financial organisations

Most of us take the easy option with our finances; we stick with the same bank account, we buy travel insurance through a travel agent and we use the same credit card both in the high street and abroad. All these poor financial decisions cost us money and mean we're not getting the best deal.

Sorting out our finances is usually high on our new-year resolutions list, yet when it comes to it most of us don't know where to start. The problem is there's no one-size-fits-all financial product and as a quarter of us tend to rely on financial advice from friends and family you can never be sure you're getting the right deal *for you*.

What do you want and need?

If you were doing a weekend of DIY you'd check you had the right tools for the job first, so when it comes to money matters you should check if there's anything missing or that needs replacing in your financial toolkit. Those *must-have* basics include:

A bank account

Ninety per cent of us have at least one bank account, yet the Office of Fair Trading say less than 10 per cent of us have moved our account over the past year.

What should you look for? Make a list of what you want. Most of us need some form of overdraft; or if your salary is paid in you might benefit from an account that pays a bonus or incentive if you credit a certain amount, say £1,000 each month; and if you rarely use cash but pay by debit card you could look for an account that offers 'cash-back' on card purchases.

A savings account

Whatever the interest rate is doing, you still need something put away for a rainy day. If, say, you're made redundant, the car breaks down or you get a big bill, ideally you should have money set aside to cover it rather than resorting to loans or credit cards. If you can, stash away around three to six months' salary, in an instant access account. If you haven't already used up your ISA (Individual Savings Account) allowance, this is the one to go for, as many offer instant access with no minimum pay-in and you can squirrel away £3,600 a year tax-free (£5,100 from 2010).

A credit card

Clearly not *essential*, but a credit card offers up to fifty-nine days' interest-free credit; so it's cheaper than using your overdraft. Get the right one and you can use it abroad without being clobbered for extra 'loading' charges. A 'loading' charge is the commission your credit card company pockets for allowing you to use your card abroad; it can be as much as 2.75 per cent, which works out at £2.75 on every £100 you spend.

As credit cards have different benefits it's often worth having more than one. So, for example, one for using abroad that does not incur a loading fee, and one for daily spending that offers a high rate of cash-back – providing you're able to clear the bill each month, otherwise any cash-back will be wiped out with interest charges.

Never have a store card unless you're absolutely sure you can *always* clear the bill each month. Most charge around 30 per cent interest a year; although savvy shoppers can benefit from any introductory discount on purchases by taking one out, clearing the bill and then cancelling the account.

Can't clear your card?

Go for a card offering the longest 0 per cent balance transfer deal you can find, enabling you to chip away at the amount you owe, without incurring further interest. These deals aren't as good as they once were, with many companies now charging balance transfer fees of up to 3 per cent on the debt you transfer across. That works out at £60 if you're transferring across a £2,000 debt, for example, but if securing the 0 per cent deal means you'll save more than that £60 in monthly interest charges, it's worth doing.

Most 0 per cent deals only hold for a limited time before reverting to a standard, much higher, interest rate. If you think you're likely to forget when your deal ends and get clobbered for interest at the full rate, or you can't secure a 0 per cent deal, go for the lowest long-term deal you can. Although you'll be paying interest on the money you owe, it will still be less than the average 18 per cent credit card rate, and many of these deals last until your debt is paid off.

Mortgages

This is a tricky one to cover, as the mortgage market is constantly changing; from the days of being able to get 125 per cent mortgages, lenders have since become much more fussy about who they lend to and how much they'll offer. Many of the lowest rate deals are now only available if you're able to put down a substantial deposit, typically around 20 per cent, or have built up substantial equity in your existing property.

Another important thing to remember is that there's no one-size-fits-all mortgage, and what's right for your neighbour or best friend won't necessarily be the best deal for you. Finding the right mortgage is one area where it's really worth seeking specialist financial advice and getting a mortgage broker on board to help you.

When choosing a mortgage broker one of the most important things to find out is whether they cover the *whole* market. This basically means they should look at all the deals available rather than a restricted selection. Also ask how they're paid: this means whether they charge a fee for their time or are paid a commission from the lender you decide to go with.

To find a good broker I'd always suggest going on recommendation, but if you can't, keep your eyes and ears open for companies that are regularly interviewed on news programmes or quoted in the press, as opposed to just randomly doing an internet search. And do check the Financial Services Authority's website to ensure any firm offering advice is regulated – there's more on this further on in the chapter.

As a good starting point, get an idea of the deals available by looking at the financial website www.moneyfacts.co.uk. Click on the mortgage link and you can see the current top mortgage deals along with any terms, conditions and fees. You can also click on different options, say if you want a three- or five-year fixed deal, or use its mortgage search facility to see what options it comes up with to suit you, your pocket and lifestyle.

It's also worth looking at the Financial Services Authority's website, which has a mortgage calculator where you can work out exactly how much your mortgage payments will be depending on how much you borrow and based on different interest rates. Go to www.moneymadeclear.fsa.gov.uk and click on the mortgage calculator section.

Remember, when comparing deals it's not just about looking at the interest rate, there's often other fees such as arrangement fees to be added on. (There's more on how to understand the different rates further on in this chapter.) Most lenders will usually offer to add any charges to your mortgage loan, but this can then mean you're repaying interest on this for the next twenty-five years.

Once you've got a mortgage, if you have spare cash at the end of the month or get a big bonus from work it's worth considering 'overpaying' on your mortgage. This means paying off a chunk of your mortgage rather than sticking the money into a savings account. Generally the interest you'll pay on your mortgage will outweigh any benefit you'd get from burying the money away. Check first that your mortgage deal allows this, though, as some lenders have a maximum amount you can overpay.

How to get the best deals

Spotted a headline-grabbing cheap rate on a credit card or low mortgage deal?

But how much will you really be paying? You'll need to know your APRs from your AERs for this one. They may look confusing but they are actually designed to give you an accurate idea of just how much you'll be paying or receiving in the way of interest once any charges have been taken into account.

Basically, an APR is the annual percentage rate; it's the rate to look for when you're borrowing money and you'll see it quoted alongside loans, mortgages and credit cards. It helps you compare the total cost of borrowing, including not only the interest rate, but any fees or charges too. So let's say one lender is offering what looks like a low mortgage rate, but charging a £500 arrangement fee, while another has a slightly higher rate but with no fee, then the APR takes all this into account, making it easier to compare the two deals.

An AER is the annual equivalent rate and basically the rate to look for when working out how much interest you'll get on your savings.

Even if your application is successful you still may not get those elusive headline-grabbing rates; the reason being that many deals advertised quote *typical APRs* (for the annual interest rate) and are 'priced according to risk'. What this means is that the *actual* rate you'll get depends on your credit rating; in other words whether you're likely to be a good or bad risk customer. When a lender looks at your credit file, if they don't feel you're a good enough bet for the 0 per cent or whatever rate they're advertising, you're likely to be offered a *similar* deal but on a higher rate.

Each lender carries out its own credit scoring on you before saying yes or no and you'll never get to find out why you're turned down. So to ensure you get the best deals you can, you must make sure your credit record is as squeaky clean as possible. It's a bit like sending in your CV for a job; you tweak it and check it's relevant for each job; so when you're about to apply for credit, check your credit file presents you in the best possible way.

How to check your credit file

Get a copy of your file from all three credit reference agencies *before* applying for credit. If the information held about you is wrong, your application could be rejected. Getting your file first means you've got the chance to correct it.

It costs £2 a time and it's worth getting a copy from all three agencies, as you won't know which lenders use which one. They are:

- Experian – 0844 481 8000 www.experian.co.uk
- Equifax – 0870 010 0583 www.equifax.co.uk
- Callcredit – 0113 244 1555 www.callcredit.co.uk

Once you've got your file, look on it for any cards, loans or accounts you're not familiar with, and if you find anything suspicious contact the relevant organisation for more details. Banks want customers who'll make money for them; if you're a model customer clearing your credit cards every month and never going overdrawn you may still be rejected. Credit card companies are now cherry-picking customers and turning down new credit card applications at the rate of eighteen thousand a day.

A savvy consumer's story

Turned down for credit but never a penny overdrawn ... This story isn't uncommon, and with lenders actively looking for ways to make money from customers you may be rejected simply because your credit history is too good.

'I applied for a new credit card after being a second-card-holder on my ex-partner's account. At the time I had my own house, was in full-time employment, had a bank account that was always in credit, several savings accounts and never owed a penny in my life.

Every time I went in a shop I was offered store cards, yet I was rejected by the first credit card company I applied to. I was really upset and worried. I applied for my credit file, which was up to date, and as my ex-partner hadn't owed money either I couldn't understand what was wrong. That's until I learned that sometimes you can't get credit simply because a card company doesn't think you're going to make money for them.

I had no way of finding out *why* I'd been rejected, so I applied for another card with another company the next day – and success. A week later I had my new card and constantly find they're raising my limit, even though I never go anywhere near it.'

Constantly raising your credit limit is a potential money spinner on the part of the credit card companies; they're hoping you'll use your card to spend more and then can't afford to pay it all back so they'll be able to pile on some interest. If you find your limit is being constantly raised, ask for it to be capped or even lowered.

Credit file clean up

You need your file looking clean and sparkling, but there's no quick-fix solution. If you've got a history of credit problems and mortgage arrears you can't wave a magic wand and wipe the slate clean overnight. Watch out for companies charging you to 'clean up' your file. They'll pocket your money but do nothing more than you can do yourself for free. Here's what you can do to boost your chances of getting the best financial deals:

Get yourself on the electoral roll

If you've just moved house, speak to your local council and get your name registered as soon as you can. Lenders like continuity, so they'll want to know that your name and address show up on the electoral roll – if not, it could mean your credit application is rejected. This is why, even if you've just moved house, it's worth trying to get on the electoral roll as soon as possible. Ask to be excluded from the version that can be used by junk-mail companies for marketing purposes.

Don't apply for credit 'just to see if you can get it'

Every time a lender looks at your file it leaves a 'footprint'. Enough of these and other lenders may wonder why you're so desperate for credit; in other words, if they loan you money will you ever pay it back?

Explain why you've had mortgage arrears or financial problems

You can have notes put on your file to explain why you fell into arrears with the mortgage payments, for example if you lost your job or split with your partner.

Close down old credit card or bank accounts

If you don't use them, close them, and ask for written confirmation when this is done. If you've got five unused credit cards on your file with potential credit of up to £10,000 on each, a prospective lender may be cagey about lending you money in case you max-out your existing credit facility and can't repay.

Check you're not linked to an ex

Check your credit file isn't still linked to an ex or someone you've had joint credit with in the past. Unless you ask the credit reference agencies to break these links when circumstances change, future applications could be tarnished by any debts the other person runs up.

Lenders don't like change

Always apply for credit *before* any changes that will show up on your file, like getting married (possible name change) or moving house.

Financial advice and who to trust to give it

Your bank will offer advice but will naturally want to flog you its own policies, products and cards. Can you imagine going into HSBC to ask about mortgages and finding they suggest you go to the Halifax or Lloyds TSB because they've got a better deal? It just wouldn't happen, which is why you need to be wary when banks offer you an opportunity to sit down with a money adviser and talk through your financial situation. While it sounds like free money advice, to the bank it's a potential chance to flog you a new product or policy.

Independent financial advice

An Independent Financial Adviser is what it says on the tin: someone who's not tied or affiliated to any one company, so they can trawl the financial marketplace to find the best products for you.

Having said that, if they earn commission on products they sell (as opposed to you paying an upfront fee for their advice) there's always the chance that they *could* be swayed into suggesting products that give the biggest commission. So now they must tell you exactly how much commission they stand to get if you sign up for products or policies on their advice. More on that below.

Finding a financial adviser – where to start?

As with any service, if you can find someone who's been recommended to you, you've got a good starting point. Financial advisers are regulated by the Financial Services Authority, so you can check if an adviser is regulated using the FSA's website at www.fsa.gov.uk or by calling them on 0300 500 5000. If an adviser isn't regulated and things go wrong, it's much harder, if not almost impossible, to get your money back.

A good site for tracking down a financial adviser in your area is www.unbiased.co.uk, which lists over nine thousand independent financial advisers across the country. Put in your postcode and what you want advice on and it comes up with contacts for locally based advisers, though it is still worth double-checking their FSA regulation.

Do I pay for advice?

Independent Financial Advisers (IFAs) are paid in two ways: they can earn commission on products they sell or charge an upfront fee for their time and advice.

As a rough guide, upfront fees can be anything from around £80 an hour to over £200, depending on where you live and the type of advice you need. If, on the other hand, there's no fee to pay but your adviser is making their money from commission, they have to tell you how much they're getting. Ask to see their *Key Facts* document; this must list all the charges.

If you're not happy with the advice given and have already complained to the company concerned, you can contact the Financial Ombudsman Service (www.fos.gov.uk), who will investigate complaints about poor financial advice for consumers, *providing* your adviser is regulated by the FSA.

Review your finances regularly (make sure you're still getting the best deal)

Just because five years ago you shopped around for the best deal on your savings, mortgage or credit card, it doesn't mean it's *still* the best deal on the market. Rates chop and change, and some lenders offer introductory rates, then later revert to less appealing ones, but they hope you won't notice and will stick with the same product.

Review your products regularly and always, *always,* shop around when your car, home, pet or travel insurance is due. Don't get lazy and just renew automatically or, worse still, agree to have the money taken from your account by an ongoing annual direct debit. Insurers are particularly keen on this one as they rely on you not being bothered to shop around and leaving it too late, and once they've got your agreement to this kind of direct debit they can happily help themselves to your money year after year.

Don't forget to negotiate

Just as you would in a shop, if you're looking around for the best financial deal ask your lender what it can do for you, and see whether it will undercut a competitor's deal. You may be hugely surprised to know that *some* lenders will either reduce or increase rates if they think they're going to lose customers.

Being blunt, this does depend on how much they can make from you, but if you prefer the convenience of sticking with an existing lender but want a better deal, do your homework and ask if it will price-match before you consider switching.

Unpaid debts

We've all got some level of debt; whether in the form of a mortgage loan, credit cards, overdraft with the bank or a personal loan for a car, kitchen or holiday. Borrowing money is fine, but it's when you can't keep up the repayments, fall into arrears with your mortgage or are regularly extending your overdraft that it becomes time to take action – before what was once a manageable debt escalates into one that you're constantly worried about and can't afford to pay.

Debt isn't just something that affects those on lower incomes; for many people it's triggered by an unexpected life change such as a relationship break-up, falling ill or losing your job. Faced with debts you can't pay, the most important thing is *not* to ignore them. Telling lenders as soon as you start having problems means they'll often be more sympathetic than if you ignore letters for months before finally facing up to what, by then, will be a much bigger debt.

Facing up to your debts

- Don't ignore them. Work out how much money you've got coming in each month and how much you can realistically afford to pay towards any debts.
- Contact everyone you owe money to, explaining the situation and telling them how much you can afford to pay.

- Ask for any interest to be frozen so you've a chance to start repaying the debt.

- Don't feel pushed into agreeing to pay more than you can afford. If you need more advice or help contacting lenders, speak to your local Citizens Advice (www.citizensadvice.org.uk), or call National Debtline (www.nationaldebtline.co.uk/0808 808 4000) or the Consumer Credit Counselling Service (www.cccs.co.uk/ 0800 138 1111). Advice from any of these organisations is free.

- Don't pay for debt advice or approach 'debt management' companies who will want payment for negotiating reduced payments on your behalf.

But are the debts yours?

Being contacted for someone else's debts is becoming increasingly common. The Credit Services Association, which represents most of the country's debt recovery agencies, is currently chasing over twenty million cases – worth over fifteen billion pounds. Because of the sheer volume of unpaid debts and the problems tracing people, a trick used by some debt recovery agencies is to contact people with the same or similar name as the debtor.

If you're contacted about a supposed debt in your name that you can't ever remember owing, ask for proof you owe the money. The person claiming the debt must *prove* you owe it, and the easiest way is by producing a copy of your original signed credit agreement. This is what you (or whoever applied for the credit) will have signed to get the store card, credit card, car finance or whatever.

It is also worth getting a copy of your credit file from all three credit reference agencies to check the details are correct. Do give them as much information as you can, including your addresses over the past six years, as without all the information your file may be incomplete and there's a chance genuine debts may not show up.

If you're having problems with a debt recovery agency or feel they're harassing you, check if they're a member of the Credit

Services Association, as members must adhere to a code of practice. You can also contact the Office of Fair Trading (OFT), as anyone collecting debts must have a credit license, issued by the OFT, and the OFT has the power to revoke the license if a company engages in bad practice.

How long can you be chased for debts?

If you owe money on store cards, credit cards, mail order, personal loans and overdrafts, you can't be taken to court beyond a six-year time limit, under the Limitation Act 1980. *But* the six-year time limit starts from the date of the last communication, *not* when the debt first occurred. So if a debt recovery agency can prove it's written to you on several occasions but you've just ignored the letters, the six-year limit starts from the date of their last communication, not the date you took on the debt.

This applies to what's known as 'unsecured' debts; typically your store cards, personal loans, etc; it's called unsecured because quite literally the lump of debt isn't attached to anything – you can't lose your home if you don't pay up. Whereas 'secured' debt is, as it sounds, secured against something, typically your home, which means if you don't keep up the repayments you could lose the roof over your head.

Mortgage debt

With mortgages, lenders legally have twelve years (across England and Wales) to contact you about seeking repayment for any money you owe. This typically happens if your home is repossessed and sold for less than the value of your original loan. In this case your ex-lender will then pursue you for this shortfall, plus interest, plus any legal and estate agent's fees.

Having said that, members of the Council of Mortgage Lenders, which represent most major lenders, signed a voluntary agreement back in 2000, which means if you've not been contacted by your lender within six years from the date of sale then you won't be liable for any shortfall.

For any mortgages taken out *after* October 2004, when the Financial Services Authority took on mortgage regulation, there's a six-year limit for chasing up mortgage debts. But while lenders are expected to *start* the chasing process within the six years, it's not necessarily the full recovery of the debt that must take place within that time frame.

Repossession – what happens next

Many people mistakenly believe that by giving back the keys and walking away, their property will be sold and they're free to crack on with the rest of their lives. This isn't the case, as lenders will try all they can to recover the money, often many years down the line, and with joint mortgages they will come after whoever they can find first for the debt, as this story illustrates.

'I bought a house with a friend of mine but after a couple of years he lost his job and started to have money problems, so he moved out to live with friends. I was struggling to pay the mortgage myself and contacted the lender. They said I was liable for the full mortgage payment and I ended up having to sell the stuff he'd left behind to try to pay the mortgage. I couldn't trace my friend and when the lender threatened repossession I was horrified to discover I could be facing a shortfall on the mortgage and that my lender wasn't actively chasing my friend for the money. I'd assumed that, being a joint mortgage, we'd both be liable, but it was a case of whoever they could find first to foot the bill.'

Debt collectors and bailiffs – what can they do?

People get confused between debt collectors and bailiffs and think they're one and the same thing. They're not. Neither have the automatic right to break into your property and you don't *have* to answer the door to them.

In some very specific cases bailiffs *may* be able to force entry for such reasons as recovering payment for criminal fines or unpaid tax bills.

Debt collectors

Debt collectors usually work on behalf of the company you owe money to, so for example that could be your credit card company, mobile phone provider or utility supplier.

If you continue to ignore requests for payment, the 'debt' will usually pass to the company's internal debt collection department. Or it may 'sell' on the debt to a third party debt recovery (or debt collection) agency.

Someone from either the original company's debt recovery department or the independent agency will ring you, write to you and finally turn up on your doorstep to try to agree some form of repayment with you, which can include reduced instalments.

If this doesn't work, you can be taken to court for the debt and a county court judgement (CCJ) will be made against you. This is basically a court order that demands that you pay the money.

If you miss a payment on this judgement, the person you owe money to can set up what's known as a 'warrant of execution', which means the county court may then send out bailiffs. They'll need to give you seven days' notice of their visit, so you can stop this by contacting the court and asking them to suspend the warrant, but this will mean agreeing to repay the money.

(For more specialised advice about your specific situation or debts, call the National Debtline on 0808 808 4000 or the Consumer Credit Counselling Service on 0800 138 1111.)

Bailiffs

Unlike in the movies, bailiffs can't come along and break down your door. They have to gain what's called 'peaceable entry'. This means they can only come in if you've left a door or window unlocked or invite them in. Bailiffs usually know their rights and may try various tactics to get in, say, asking to come in for a 'chat'.

If they've gained 'peaceable entry' on their first visit they can make what's known as a 'walking possession agreement'; basically a list of items that *could* be taken and sold to recover the debt. These can't include any goods directly related to your work or your basic household essentials, like a washing machine or a fridge. If you still don't make payment, on a subsequent visit they *can* force entry to seize these goods, but only providing their first visit was a 'peaceable' one. It is also worth knowing that jointly owned goods can be at risk, providing the debtor is a part owner.

If, after turning up a couple of times, the bailiffs don't get any response, they can ask the court to impose other ways of recovering the debt. This can include a 'charging order' on your property, which means any debt plus interest and fees will be recovered as and when the property is sold.

Settling debts: negotiating a full and final settlement

This means negotiating a reduced lump-sum payment in return for the rest of the debt being written off. Any full and final settlement should be negotiated with your original lender; or debt recovery agency, if the original debt has since been sold to a third party debt recovery agency. Tell them what you're prepared to pay as a *full and final settlement*. Don't try to agree a reduced settlement figure with the bailiffs or debt collectors on the doorstep.

Obviously any offer you make doesn't have to be accepted, but from a lender's viewpoint something is better than nothing; particularly if there's the risk of you going bankrupt as then they're unlikely to see a penny of any money owed. You've got to be tough here and stand your ground, as naturally they'll want to get as much from you as they can and part of their job is sorting out the 'can't pays' from the 'won't pays'.

If your offer is accepted, get this in writing *before* making any payment.

Houses and property

Your home is the most expensive purchase you'll ever make, yet we spend less time choosing it than we do measuring up for the curtains. Yes, research shows we spend a mere seventeen minutes choosing our home and nearly an hour deciding on which curtains to hang in it.

House prices and even rental rates are *always* worth negotiating on. While it's said a good property sells close to its asking price, there's always room for negotiation. And not just on the property price – on all those additional costs you face when buying or selling, too, including estate agents' and solicitors' fees.

While there's a whole book to write on how to get the best deal in the property market, this chapter is intended as a whistle-stop tour through some of the main areas where you can negotiate, with advice on how to do it.

Selling your home

While there are lots of ways in which you can sell your home – including using websites and even sticking a board in the front garden yourself – most people still rely on an estate agent to do the job for them.

Estate agents

They get a rough ride at times and there's a mixed bag out there – some good, some bad – but find a good agent and they can secure the best price and sell your home in double quick time.

Estate agents' fees aren't cheap. Typically they'll charge around 1.5 per cent commission to sell your property; that's £3,000 on a £200,000 property, and if you want several agents to market it, you're looking at paying around 2.5 per cent commission.

Finding a good agent

- Before you start, get a rough idea of how much your property is worth. There are lots of websites where you can type in your postcode to find details of how much properties in your area have recently sold for, such as www.nethouseprices.com.

- Go through the property pages in your local paper to check prices and call several agents, posing as a buyer. Mystery shop them to see how friendly, efficient and knowledgeable they are. Do you feel they'd be good at selling your property?

- Are they a member of the National Association of Estate Agents? If so, this means you've got comeback if you're unhappy with their service.

- Get valuations from at least three agents and go for a mix of both big-name chains and local companies, who may have more expert local knowledge.

- Compare the commission rates they're charging along with any lock-in time and *negotiate*. Play one agent off against the other, as they'll all want your business. The smaller independent companies will often have more power to agree a discount than the nationwide chains, who may need to get approval from head office.

- Don't just choose the agent who gives the highest valuation, as this may not be achievable. If one agent values your property much higher than the rest, ask the reason why.

- Once your property is on their books, mystery shop them again. Get a friend to call up and find how good they are at marketing your property. If you feel they've done a poor job, come clean and challenge them.

What's the best deal?

It's finding an agent to sell your home in the shortest time for the best price.

While agency fees are important, you've got to decide whether it's worth paying a slightly higher level of commission to an agent who can get you a quick sale at the price you want. Or would you rather go with a cheaper agent and risk your property sitting on its books for six months with barely a viewing?

Sue's savyy stories – it happened to me

I remember being on a radio consumer programme when a lady rang in complaining her estate agent had ripped her off. She claimed he'd taken the commission but hardly done any work for the money.

She went on to tell the full story, which was that she'd signed with an agent on the Friday, and by Sunday had two viewings; one of which resulted in an offer which she'd accepted. Her gripe? She felt the agent hadn't really *earned* the money she was paying.

I asked her whether she'd rather pay the same commission to an agent who'd got her twenty viewings in a month but with no offers. Sometimes it *can* seem you're paying an agent for what amounts to just a few hours' work if your property sells quickly, *but* the way to look at it is that you're paying for their *experience* and *knowledge*, hence they've been able to secure the right buyer at the best price quicker than their competitors.

Selling online

Over 80 per cent of house hunters start looking online, but most properties advertised on the net are with agents with both a high-street and online outlet.

It *is* possible to cut costs by not using an agent, and advertising your property yourself. This is best done online, where there are lots of websites offering a service where you upload your own photos and write your own description, all for around a few hundred pounds. On the plus side, yes, it's much cheaper than estate agents' fees, but remember you'll be the one in charge of arranging viewings, answering vendors' questions and negotiating on the price, rather than relying on an agent.

If *you're* responsible for taking buyers round, think about how you're going to *sell* your property. Simply taking someone round and pointing out which room is which *is not* the key to getting the best price. Watch how they do it on those TV property shows; it's all about selling a lifestyle, so think of all the positives (don't mention the negatives) and actively point out things you want buyers to notice in each room. Make sure you know basic details, too, like the price of your bills and which band of council tax you're on; these are all things a buyer will want to know and will make you seem more knowledgeable about your property.

Tricks to get the best price for your property *and* a quick sale

Spending a bit of cash sprucing up the place, adding a few well co-ordinated accessories and giving it a thorough de-clutter can potentially boost your selling price by thousands and secure a quick sale.

Put yourself in the buyers' shoes. If you were looking to knock the price down, what reasons would you give? Get an honest friend to come round and tell you the problems or faults they notice; we get so used to living in our homes we sometimes don't notice the obvious.

- Tidy up. You'd be amazed how many people leave the place in a complete tip for potential buyers – I once had to walk over piles of dirty clothes on the floor. And make sure you clean the bathroom and loo, too.

- Get unsightly jobs fixed, otherwise buyers will use any faults to try to negotiate a lower price.

- De-personalise your property. Paint walls a warm but neutral colour like a classic magnolia. You want buyers to believe they could live there, not feel they'd be moving into 'your' home.

- Rooms should do what they say. So a third bedroom should have a bed in it, not look like a junk room, and the dining room shouldn't have been turned into a temporary office.

- Check your property's 'kerbside' appeal. Most buyers drive past a property to check it out before arranging a viewing. If your front garden's full of weeds, the bins are overflowing, the windows are grubby and the driveway looks like a used parking lot, they won't come back.

- Check the place *smells* good; particularly if you've got pets or you're a smoker.

- If you're caught out by a sudden instant offer, have a fall-back position. This means saying you need to talk it over with your husband/wife/partner, etc. – this buys you time and means you won't be rushed into making an on-the-spot decision.

Home staging

You can pay companies to give your property the 'show home' look, but the cheapest way is to do it yourself. Look at the houses in glossy magazines to get ideas; remember nobody *actually lives* like this, but when selling you've got to 'dress' your property to make it appeal and get the best price. Or do you know anyone who's started out in interior design who'd give you a couple of hours of their time in exchange for using photos of your property's 'before' and 'after' look on their website?

Having coffee brewing for prospective clients is now somewhat outdated and predictable. What gives a good impression are things like having scented candles burning around the house, having the dining table laid for dinner, complete with a bottle of champagne on ice (if it's summer, do this on the patio ready for an evening's 'al fresco' dining), and keep the house totally free from clutter. Try to arrange viewings for the brightest time of day so potential buyers see your property at its best.

Buying a property

This time round you're not paying the estate agent's bill, but you still need to choose your agent carefully. You don't want someone who will send you everything on their books regardless of your price or location.

Be everyone's favourite buyer. Get your finance in place – that means talking to lenders first, so you know what you can afford before you consider making an offer. If you're a first-time buyer or chain-free, tell an agent this as this puts you in a more favourable position.

How much to offer?

Remember the asking price may have been pitched just that little bit higher in anticipation of lower offers. Go in with too high an opening offer and you may find there's not much room for further negotiation, or if your initial offer is accepted you could kick yourself for not offering less.

Before you make an offer, find out how long the property has been on the market and if there have been any offers. This is something you can ask the vendors as many will often let details like this slip, whereas an agent will be much more savvy about how much to tell you. It is also worth trying to catch the neighbours to see if they can fill you in on any more details. The longer it's been on the market, the potentially lower your offer can be.

As a very rough guide, going in at around 10 per cent lower than the asking price is OK, unless the property needs substantial work doing; in which case you should get an accurate idea of costs in the form of quotes that you can show the vendors when negotiating on price.

Sue's savvy stories – it happened to me

Before you consider making an offer, unearth the stories the estate agent or homeowner won't tell you. This usually means visiting the property at different times of the day and asking lots of questions. If you don't ask, they may not volunteer extra information.

A few years ago I was house hunting and arranged a viewing on what I thought was a property that ticked all the boxes. Standing in the garden on a sunny Sunday morning chatting with the owner, we were suddenly drowned out by the sound of loud drumming coming from her neighbour's house.

The lady in question seemed horribly embarrassed about this and said it was the first time it had happened. I thought I'd carry out my own investigation and drove past the property a couple of times on future weekends, only to hear her over-eager neighbour in the throes of a full practice again, and again ...

Negotiating on the price

It may be your biggest purchase, but most of us don't negotiate with a strategy in place. As with any request for a discount, say *why* you want a reduction in the price. The more plausible the reason, the more chance you've got of succeeding.

- *Show you know what you're talking about* – let the vendor know you've viewed lots of properties, are clued up on the local market and know the price of similar properties in the area. This shows you won't be easily put off.

- *Play hard to get* – never be too keen. On your first viewing, however excited you are at discovering your 'dream' home, don't let it show. If an agent or vendor picks up on how keen you are, they may stick to the original asking price.

- *Take your time* – don't rush into making an offer. You'll usually get a call from the agent shortly after viewing a property to see what you think. Take this opportunity to point out any faults or problems.

- *Cut stamp duty fees* – you've got to be careful on this and play by the rules. The tax office takes a dim view of anyone deliberately trying to avoid paying stamp duty, but if the property has an asking price that's borderline on the next stamp duty bracket – which could mean a huge hike in fees – it's worth trying to negotiate a price under this and paying cash for a few extras like, say, the kitchen appliances.

- *Negotiate face to face* – the reason for this is you're talking potential big money discounts and you'll be able to gauge their reaction better this way. It's easier to bluff on the phone so, providing you feel confident enough, make an appointment to see the agent. And if they imply that your offer could be refused, don't instantly up it. This looks desperate.

HIPs (Home Information Packs)

This is one area where it can be hard to negotiate a better deal.

HIPs (Home Information Packs) have been gradually phased in since August 2007 according to the size of a property, and anyone marketing their property in England and Wales now needs one. A HIP is like a property CV for buyers. There's stuff in there about how energy efficient the place is, along with practical details like how much the council tax costs and parking arrangements. It's basically much of the paperwork done upfront and is paid for by the home owner.

The key word here is 'marketing', and even a sign stuck outside your property counts as marketing, so don't think you can get away without having a HIP if you're not advertising through an agent. If you don't 'market' your property, you don't need a HIP, but unless you're prepared to rely on the off chance that a random stranger comes knocking on your door wanting to buy, you'll have a job to (legally) avoid a HIP.

Some agents will cover the cost for you, though check you're not paying for the cost through any other charges, like, say, a higher commission rate for selling.

Conveyancing fees

Conveyancing is basically the legal side of buying and selling property and it's what most people pay a solicitor to do for them. There's nothing to stop you doing the job yourself, but it can be time consuming without the relevant expertise.

So, find a company that offers a fixed-fee service to do the buying, selling or both for you. Agents will often recommend a local firm they have a deal with, but while this can seem the easy option, shop around on price first.

There are some legal firms that offer a 'remote' conveyancing service, which often means you don't actually get the chance to sit down opposite someone to discuss the finer points of the property sale. This can be difficult; I heard of one case where the buyer was reduced to having to borrow the receptionist's head-set to talk to the solicitor in the office two floors above when they didn't understand something about the property sale, but the service they'd paid for didn't include a sit-down meeting.

Letting property

Letting property isn't only about investment. People often let out of necessity; becoming 'accidental landlords', if you like – if, say, they can't sell their property or are temporarily moving away, even going abroad, but want a place to come back to. One of the first decisions to make is whether you're going to hand over the running of the place to an agent or handle the let yourself.

DIY or an agency?

When I've let property I've done it privately and never used an agent; the reason being that while some agents do their job properly, I think for some they consider lettings 'easy money' in terms of getting commission every month for quite simply doing nothing.

Managing a let yourself takes time and you've got to be prepared for unexpected call-outs if, say, there's a problem and you've got to arrange a plumber to fix an emergency leak. But on the plus side it means you're in control and always know what's going on, as you could even arrange to pop round to collect the rent each month. On average you'll save around 12–15 per cent of your rental income doing it yourself.

Finding tenants privately

This is where agents often have the upper hand, as they've got the shop front and online presence to reach a wide market. If you're doing it privately, as well as advertising in local papers advertise on work noticeboards. I used to contact large multi-national companies in the area where my property was based, as they'd often pass the details to employees who'd just moved to the area or were on secondment. This has the added bonus that they're professional people with a job and regular income, although naturally you still need to check out references.

Guaranteed rent schemes

As a landlord, getting long-term tenants and regular rent can be a headache. And when the market slows you may find you've got to lower your rent to get tenants in.

Some property agents offer 'guaranteed rent' schemes. This means you're paid a regular 'pay packet' each month, regardless of whether your property sits empty or not. While this sounds like a 'win-win' situation, it *can* mean you're one step removed from your property, as in effect you're letting your property to the agent, who in turn sub-lets to tenants. If there's a problem you could be the last to know. But depending on the property market, if tenants are getting harder to come by it *can* be worth doing. So what do you need to think about?

- Rental income is usually substantially reduced, typically 30 per cent less than the 'going rate'.

- What you've got to work out is whether having a lower but regular rental income all year round is better than, say, one month of the property sitting empty every year while you're hunting for tenants, but also a higher rate for the rest of the year.

- Always get any contracts checked thoroughly by a solicitor and find out if there's a minimum contract term in place.

Being a tenant

Some rents are fixed and some landlords are prepared to be flexible on price. Put it this way, unless they've got potential tenants crawling out of the woodwork they would probably rather let the property for a year or longer at a discounted rate than have it sitting empty for a couple of months. You're in a better haggling position if the property's sitting empty.

Sue's savvy stories – it happened to me

I'd been renting a house through a property agent for just over a year when the agent sold up, taking early retirement. My landlord was considering using another agent but I pointed out that, having rented the place for over a year, I'd always been a good tenant and if we arranged it privately he'd save on agency fees. I then asked if we could split the difference he'd save by doing this, which would be about £50 per month.

At first he seemed really taken aback and clearly thought I had a right cheek asking, *but* the very next day he rang back agreeing to the £25 reduction.

Landlords want long-term reliable tenants, so 'sell' yourself as the perfect tenant. Tips to negotiate a lower rent include asking to take the property unfurnished. Many furnished places only have the basics, so if you've got your own furniture ask if the landlord will let unfurnished, which should work out cheaper. If you've found a property you like but feel the rent is higher than the market rate, check prices locally. It is worth emailing your prospective landlord examples of other properties in the area that are going for less, to see if they'll budge.

While as a tenant you're responsible for looking after the place, offering to do *extra* jobs that could otherwise cost the landlord money may help you secure a discount too, for example painting the inside or outside of the property.

Avoiding the cowboys (builders, plumbers, garages and paying for services)

Dealing with small businesses and sole traders means adopting a different, more personable approach, compared with the way you might handle negotiations with a larger, more impersonal company.

If you're arranging for someone to do work in your home, say a builder, plumber or electrician, for example, you're effectively taking on the role of their 'employer'. So telling them what's needed and negotiating both price and contract terms is down to you. Paying someone to do a job you can't do, or don't know how to do yourself, can make you feel on the back foot; but you're the one paying the bill so *you* need to take control.

At the garage it's often the same story; we feel out of our comfort zone as we need a job done, can't do it ourselves and are reliant on someone else's expertise. And it's often the case that we're so desperate to get the car fixed, that leaky washing machine mended or those tiles on the roof fixed, etc., that we don't ask questions and negotiate the way we would in the high street.

So whether you want a new conservatory built, to have the car serviced or get the central heating fixed, how can you make sure you get value for money?

This chapter's about making sure the price you're given is the one you pay. It's about knowing how to spot a genuine trader from a cowboy and the tricks to watch out for, like adding VAT to the bill when they shouldn't be charging it in the first place ...

Builders, plumbers, electricians, decorators (and anyone else doing work in your home)

You might feel the ultimate deal is being able to do the job yourself, but while most of us can cope with a paintbrush, if you're planning DIY electrics, double glazing or building work you're likely to get into hot water if you don't have the relevant permission and approval for the job. Depending on what you're doing this may mean having work approved by either your local authority's building control department or, with electrics, having the job done by a qualified electrician or signed off by one.

Go ahead and bodge the job yourself and you could be out of pocket twice over; as if your work isn't up to scratch you may have to pull it down and *then* pay someone else to do it.

Go on recommendation (if you can)

If you want a job done, always ask around for recommendations. The best people I've found to do everything from fix my car to decorating and tiling have been through recommendation. And not necessarily always from friends; one of my best 'finds' was the man who fixes and services my car. He works out of a very basic garage workshop (but remember garages with coffee machines and glossy magazines in reception mean you'll pay for them with higher bills) and was recommended by a local taxi driver. Over the years I've jotted down names and numbers of tradespeople who've been suggested, 'just in case' I need to call on them.

Going it alone

If you don't know anyone for the job, look at websites like www.trustatrader.com, where you can search by area and read customers' reviews. To be listed, traders need a minimum of two years' experience and must be a member of a relevant trade organisation. Or go to www.trustmark.org.uk – a Government-endorsed site where firms are checked in a variety of areas, including health and safety, workmanship, customer satisfaction, etc., with additional checks made by Trading Standards.

'Google' the company before you call them to see what comes up. If there are articles about unhappy customers in the local papers or features on consumer programmes, you know to steer clear.

Check a company is who it says it is

Claiming to be a limited company may give the impression of being a large professional outfit, but you only need two people on the books to qualify as such. Check the company is listed at Companies House, which is where records of all the UK's limited companies are kept. You can do a free search online at www.companieshouse.gov.uk. If you want to check out their premises, bear in mind a company's registered address on the Companies House site may not be the individual's home or office address. Some companies list their accountant's address as their registered trading address.

Trade organisations

Belonging to a trade organisation can make a business look good. While membership is usually voluntary, it often means the company's been checked out and has to adhere to certain standards or they'll be struck off.

Going with a company that's backed by a recognised trade organisation also means you've got comeback if you're not happy with the job, as there'll usually be an in-house arbitration scheme.

But just because a trader *doesn't* belong to a trade organisation doesn't mean they're no good. In some cases, however good they are, the cost of high membership fees may prevent small companies from applying. Some family-run businesses that have been trading for years rely solely on reputation and recommendation rather than belonging to trade organisations.

If a trader claims to be a member of a particular trade association, call to find out if they're still a *current* member. It's not unknown for traders who let their membership lapse to keep logos and accreditation on their paperwork to boost their profile. And if it's an organisation you're not familiar with, don't be afraid to ask for more information, or call Consumer Direct or Citizens Advice to see if they've heard of them.

Turn detective and check their work

Even if someone's recommended you should always inspect their work, wherever possible. We all have different ideas of what's an acceptable standard of workmanship, so even if your friend thinks their new bathroom looks great and suggests you use the same company, take a look to make sure you'd be happy with the way it has been done.

Obviously this is relatively easy if you're looking to employ a builder or double-glazing company, but it's naturally difficult if it's a plumber or electrician as you can't usually see any work involved.

Agreeing a price

Always get written quotes from at least three different companies before committing to have any work done. Not only will this give you an idea of what's a reasonable price for the job but you'll get the benefit of three traders' expertise and advice on how to do it. Then if there's any confusion over the final price, it means you've got something on paper to produce in court.

Are you being charged an hourly rate, a daily rate or price per job? Most call-out engineers, for example, work on an hourly rate for emergency plumbing, but if you're having ongoing work done, such as a new bathroom fitted, it's best to go for a price per job. This way there's the incentive for them to get the job done rather than paying an hourly rate to someone who expects a cup of tea every hour and a ten-minute chat.

Be clear what the job involves: what's included and what's not. Who is responsible for clearing and disposing of rubbish, such as old kitchen units or building rubble? All this needs to be taken into account and written down; if not in an official contract, at least in some form of written document or quote that you keep hold of.

Agree a time limit

Agree a start and end date. Depending on the work involved the weather could play a part in this, but make sure you know how long the project *should* take. If the work can't start because you've messed up delivery dates or forgotten to order materials, you may be expected to cover the cost of any wasted days while your builder (or whoever) is unable to start work.

Staged payments

If there are materials involved, say when building a conservatory, you may be expected to make payment in stages so your builder doesn't need to fork out for all the materials themself. If this is the case it should be clear from the start how much materials and labour will cost. Don't hand over cash for random supplies without getting a receipt, and be clear when the final payment's due. You should be given time to fully inspect any work done and 'sign off' the job, so to speak, before handing over full payment.

Say no to *anyone* wanting full payment upfront for any job. Chances are they'll want cash, and in some cases will even offer to go to the bank with you. (There's more on this and other potential scams in Chapter 3.)

Don't feel embarrassed to ask to look over any work before paying up. A good tradesperson will be comfortable with this and keen to put right anything you're not happy with.

Quotes and estimates – what's the difference?

- A quote should be an all-inclusive price for the job and list VAT, if payable (see below).

- An estimate is more of an educated 'guess' as to what the job will cost. I tend to call these the 'guesstimate', as they're more likely to go up as the job goes on.

VAT (Value Added Tax)

Companies with a turnover of less than £68,000 don't need to register for VAT so they shouldn't charge it on their bills. If a company includes VAT on the bill, it must list its registered VAT number. So if you're asked to pay VAT but there's no VAT number listed, don't pay it. If you've got a company's VAT number, check they're officially registered for VAT by calling the Revenue and Customs National Advice Service on 0845 010 9000.

Asking for a discount

How much you get in the way of any reduction is likely to depend on how busy the tradesperson is and how badly they want the job. Someone who's always got plenty of work won't usually need to discount, whereas a company that's keen for a job, or just starting out, may be more prepared to negotiate.

Where you're unlikely to win is when you're desperate. If your hot water system's broken and you call up a heating engineer in a mad panic and then try and knock down the call-out charge, you're unlikely to get far as they know you need the job done and quickly.

With companies selling big-ticket items like double glazing, kitchens and bathrooms there's usually a big margin for discount. If you make a play of being indecisive or say you're getting quotes from other companies you'll often get a reduced price or an offer to price-match any existing quote you've got. This is where getting several quotes is essential as you can play one company off against another, but remember it's not just about the *cheapest* – decide which company's products are the best quality and which company you trust to do a really good job on the installation.

A ex-double-glazing salesman I used to work with told me he was able to discount up to 20 per cent on the spot without referring back to the office; and the potential discounts can be much more than that. He said as the majority of people *never ever* asked for a discount, it always meant a big fat commission for him as he'd always go in with the higher price, and the potential for a big discount for those who actually asked for it. Put it this way; if out of five customers four paid the full price and only one asked for a discount, it was worth his while to agree a bigger discount as he'd still got the full price from four of them.

And it's the same story when buying kitchens, bathrooms and other large purchases. Sales teams have targets, but in order to meet those targets they'll have a degree of flexibility on the price. If you don't sign up for that new £5,000 kitchen, they lose the sale and the commission, so better they get you to sign up for, say, £4,000 than not at all; or get you to pay the £5,000 but on interest-free credit or throw in some appliances rather than offer a discount.

With smaller businesses, offering to pay cash will usually secure a small discount, as a cash payment saves time and there's the added security of knowing they've been paid without risking rubber cheques.

Sue's savvy stories – it happened to me

When I had double glazing installed I rang several companies for quotes. The first one quoted what I thought was a high price but claimed they could get the job done quickly – though 'quickly' did seem to be an amazingly short time and I was concerned the windows would be thrown in at breakneck speed.

The second company was going to take longer, but as it was a price per job and I'd negotiated a better deal than with the first company, I was happy. But despite any discount, what clinched it was the feeling that I trusted this company, hence I chose to give them the work.

The first company, having heard nothing, as you'd expect got back in touch to offer a further reduced price (by text) and undercut their own predicted installation time.

So it just goes to show it's not always just about price but what you're getting for your money, or feel you're getting for your money, in terms of their time, workmanship and service.

Added extras will cost you

While your decorator's got the paint out, it's tempting to ask if they can just touch up the ceiling in another room. Or perhaps you ask your carpet fitter to lay the spare in your hall, *but* don't assume they're doing this as a favour. Time is money; it makes economic sense to ask them to do the work while they're already in the house but don't assume it's free. Just ask upfront if they could do whatever job you have in mind, and if so will it cost more. If you've used someone several times this is where they might be prepared to help you out at short notice or do you the odd favour, which they'd usually charge their other clients for.

Sue's savvy stories – it happened to me

Never underestimate the power of a mug of tea. Being quick to offer anyone doing work around your house a fresh brew and a plate of biscuits can go a long way. It can be the ultimate deal-clincher and mean someone doing just that little bit more than they have to.

'When my washing machine packed up I called out an engineer. We got chatting and he told me how he often got called out only to find the reason machines had packed up was down to kids' toys being poked in them or the filter never having been cleaned. He said that if the machine was under warranty, strictly speaking he was supposed to bill for his time unless the problem was an actual machine fault. "But to be honest, if they've given me a decent cup of tea and I like them I don't usually bother", he admitted. "I get paid for my day's work and don't make any more whether I charge them or not."

And when it comes to persuading someone to go that extra mile, often tea and biscuits (particularly chocolate Hobnobs) can work wonders.

My parents have always been very good in the tea and biscuit department when they've had anyone working round the house. One particular day my dad called someone out to fix the fridge, which had been playing up. A couple of mugs of tea and chocolate biscuits later he casually mentioned that the oven door was a bit loose (knowing the oven and fridge were made by the same company) and as luck would have it the man himself was now in my mum and dad's kitchen two feet away from the oven ...

So having fixed the fridge, the chap then took a look at the oven and fixed the door within minutes, free of charge.

Insurance

Check anyone working in your home is covered by public liability insurance. This protects you and your property if there's an accident. It's no good getting what you think is a great deal, then finding your plumber sticks his foot through your bedroom ceiling and tells you he's not insured so you've got to sue him for the damage.

Sue's savvy stories – it happened to me

'We get trade discount so we tend to add a bit extra on the bill.' This is not the best way to make someone give you a job but this is what one kitchen fitter told me he does with his quotes.

I'd asked about a particular kitchen range that was only available to trade. Knowing that this chap could get a discount, I asked for the price list and brochure. 'I'll give you the brochure but there are no prices in it,' he told me, saying he'd get the job priced including any discount. Basically, the story was, the more business he put their way the higher his discount. 'So as we get trade discount, say, I can get a kitchen at £3,000 instead of £5,000 for a customer, and then I'll add another £300 on the bill.' Hastily realising his mistake he tried to cover up by claiming this was only for *certain* customers.

And no, he didn't get the job.

Ask about private jobs

Many tradespeople working for an organisation will take on private work. Whether their employers would approve of them 'moonlighting' is another matter, but when asked if they do private work I've always had a quick response, with a mobile number being handed over.

While obviously the usual advice is not to go with anyone only offering a mobile number, if we're talking about someone you've already had in your home and who's done a good job I'd waive the mobile rule on this one. After all, you can hardly ring them in their 'day' job to ask about working after hours.

A few years back I had a lounge carpet laid by a major carpet store and the man offered his card at the end saying he did private work at weekends but to call his mobile for quotes. Since then I've used him a couple of times to lay carpets and flooring and while his prices were much cheaper than the 'in store' price, his work was always top quality.

Garages

Getting an all-in quote for car repairs can sometimes be difficult as there may be subsequent work that needs doing or potential faults discovered once the bonnet's up.

A good garage *should* be able to give you an idea of how much a job will cost, along with the best and worst scenarios, and you should get them to call you if they discover any other problems along the way. This puts you in control when it comes to deciding whether to go ahead with any further repairs, depending on how urgent they are. Always try to have a chat with the mechanic who'll be working on your car; this is much easier with smaller outlets as often at larger garages you'll merely be expected to leave the keys at reception.

Paying for work

Prices vary across the country and according to whether you're using a franchised dealership or independent garage.

Before paying up make sure you're given a detailed invoice listing parts, labour and VAT. If you're not happy or the price far exceeds the original quote, speak to the manager. If the situation can't be resolved and the only way to get your car back is to pay up, do so but say you're paying 'under protest' and write this on the back of your cheque and on the paperwork. This shows you are not happy and only paid up under duress in order to get your car back.

Don't refuse to pay. A garage can keep your car until full payment is made and if you take the keys and drive off without settling up you could be prosecuted for theft. If you pay by cheque or credit card it's unwise to stop payment once it's made, as once again this could be considered 'theft'.

Always trust your gut feeling

This is a vital thing to keep in mind – however good the price and credentials of any potential trader, if you don't like them or feel uncomfortable with them, don't use them.

With car repairs it's unlikely you'll spend much time with the person fixing your car, but with building work you could find you're spending most of every day sharing your home with that person, particularly if you don't work or are self-employed. So it's important that you feel confident you'll be comfortable with them being around; not dreading the moment they arrive every morning and counting down the hours until they leave.

Cancellation rights

If you've signed to order a new bathroom, fitted wardrobes or double glazing and have now decided you just don't want it or can't afford it, there's a bit of legislation that covers you called the Cancellation of Contracts made in a Consumer's Home or Place of Work etc. Regulations 2008.

Signing up at home

This legislation includes not just your own home but signing up in someone else's home, your workplace or basically anywhere other than on the trader's own business premises.

Under consumer law you've got a seven-day cooling-off period to change your mind and cancel, *providing* the goods cost over £35. It doesn't matter whether you contacted the company to arrange the visit or they turned up on your doorstep unannounced; you've still got the same seven-day cooling-off period, regardless of how they ended up sitting in your front room.

Some items are excluded from this, including signing up for mortgages, insurance products and delivery of food and drink. If you're taking out finance to cover the cost you've also got additional rights, which are listed below.

You should be given details of this cooling-off period when you sign the contract. This may either be a separate piece of paper, often headed up as 'Notice of the right to cancel', or if details are included on the contract it's got be clear and by law can't be hidden away in the teeny tiny print. If you're not given details of this right to cancel, the contract can't be enforced anyway. In the real world it can be hard to prove that you weren't given one of these, so it's worth asking for it upfront.

Signing up on trade premises

Generally you don't have the automatic right to cancel if you sign up on trade premises, so think before you sign or hand over that deposit. In *some* cases you may find a company is prepared to refund your deposit and cancel your order, providing they've not had the product specially made, but legally they don't have to do this.

If you sign up to finance as part of the deal

Signing up to a finance deal, for example interest-free credit, also entitles you to a cooling-off period under the Consumer Credit Act. Providing you signed up anywhere *other* than the trader's premises you've got five days to cancel, and the five days start the day *after* you receive the second copy of the credit agreement.

If you want to cancel, you can either use this form or write a separate letter; this should be sent to the finance company and a copy sent to the dealer within the five-day period. With letters like this it's worth sending them Recorded Signed For so you have proof they arrived.

Always take time to read any terms and conditions first. Under the Consumer Credit Act, details of any interest payable must be listed on the contract, but rates can – and do – vary, so it's down to you to read the contract and check you're happy with this.

Holidays and leisure

Your holiday may be what you've saved hard for all year, but how many of us pay the brochure price without shopping around? Since holidays and air travel have become much cheaper over the years, thanks to budget airlines and websites where you create your own trip, there's no excuse for paying up without checking you're getting the best deal.

This means finding the best flight price from the airport that suits you, going where you want, and not settling for poor-quality accommodation because the tour operator thinks they can get away with it.

And in recent times, with many holiday companies and airlines going to the wall, even if you've got a great deal, how can you make sure you're protected if the holiday company goes bust before you fly?

Protect your holiday booking

Booking your holiday early can mean good news for your pocket. The general rule is the earlier you book, the cheaper the price, as air fares will go up (due to seat availability) the closer you get to departure. But what happens to your holiday if the company you've booked with goes bust?

Package holidays

Book a package holiday through a tour operator or travel agent and you're automatically protected under the European Package Travel Regulations. A 'package holiday' doesn't necessarily have to mean a tour-rep style trip; it's just two parts of a holiday booked together at the same time. This could be, say, a flight plus accommodation, or a ferry or coach trip plus a hotel.

By law, anyone selling package holidays with a flight must be ATOL (Air Travel Organisers' Licensing) bonded. This is basically a protection scheme backed by the Civil Aviation Authority which means you'll get your money back if the travel company or airline goes bust. If you've booked through an ATOL-bonded operator, you're covered regardless of whether the booking was made in person, online or by phone.

If the airline or tour operator goes bust *before* you leave, you'll get a refund, and if you're *already* on holiday when this happens, the cost of continuing your trip and being flown home will be paid by the Civil Aviation Authority, so you won't be out of pocket.

You can check a travel company's ATOL registration at www.atol.org.uk or by calling 020 7453 6700. Check the company paperwork or website for details, as the ATOL number is usually at the bottom of the page.

The vast majority of travel agents and tour operators also belong to ABTA (The Travel Association, formerly known as the Association of British Travel Agents). Membership is voluntary but over 90 per cent of agents and operators are members. This also gives you added protection if your travel company goes bust or there's a problem with your holiday. This can be of huge benefit with accommodation-only style deals, which aren't protected by ATOL.

Booking your trip through an ABTA member also gives you added protection in the event you're disappointed with your holiday, as it will act as a go-between in any dispute you have with your tour operator or travel agent.

Flight-only bookings

These days more and more of us are opting for independent travel, which involves a whole different set of rules when it comes to protection. This is because the airlines don't have ATOL bonding, which means that when you book a flight with them directly you have less protection than with a package deal.

Tour operators selling flight-only deals (known as airline consolidators) must have ATOL protection; if you buy a flight-only deal from your travel agent you'll either be covered by ATOL (depending on who they buy the ticket from) or by buying a scheduled airline failure insurance policy.

Protect yourself – pay by credit card

The easiest and sure-fire way to ensure you'll get your money back if the airline goes bust is to pay by credit card.

This can mean paying a few pounds more on the price of your trip, as some companies impose a surcharge of around 2 per cent for credit card payments, but it's worth it as you'll get automatic protection under the Consumer Credit Act (remember good old Section 75 from Chapter 4 earlier in the book); and here's where it kicks in to help you out.

Paying by debit card doesn't automatically give you the same protection as using a credit card. Some companies, like Visa, operate their own scheme called 'chargeback', where you can make a claim through your bank if you paid by debit card, but there's a time limit for claims. Paying by cash or cheque offers you zero protection.

If you don't have a credit card you might want to consider Scheduled Airline Failure Cover. You can buy this insurance from a travel agent or insurer and it pays out for the cost of your ticket home if your airline collapses while you're abroad.

Watch for sneaky credit card companies trying to wriggle out of their responsibility

If your airline goes bust while you're away and you don't have ATOL protection or Scheduled Airline Failure Cover, you'll have to buy your own ticket home.

Buying a one-way ticket on the day will cost more than the return portion of your original ticket, but if you paid by credit card you can recover this extra cost by making a claim under Section 75 of the Consumer Credit Act once you're home, *but* there have been cases of credit card companies trying to wriggle out of coughing up.

In some cases they *may* try to get away with simply refunding the *original unused* return portion of your ticket. To explain this simply, let's say you booked a return flight to New York with Superfast Airways. You pay the £300 return fare, get there, and two days into your trip find Superfast has gone bust. You're then left to book an alternative flight home which may well cost you many times more than the original £150 return leg of your ticket, but when you get home and claim against your credit card company, it tries to offer you just £150, despite you having had to fork out the additional cost to return home.

If this happens and the credit card company won't budge, you should contact the Financial Ombudsman Service, who act as judge and jury in these matters.

Bagging the best flight deals

- Avoid school holidays if you can, as prices rocket months in advance. Easier said than done if you've got children, but try to make the most of any school closure dates to grab a long weekend break, say to Disneyland Paris, as it's loads cheaper than during the holidays.

- Be as flexible as you can. Most online sites have an option to check fares either side of your intended departure date. Sometimes a few days' difference can mean a reduction of several hundred pounds, particularly if you're looking at days either side of school holidays.

- Don't assume the big airlines can't undercut the budget ones; sometimes you'll find the likes of British Airways *are* cheaper on flights to Europe.

- If you're booking a weekday budget flight, travel at lunchtime or in mid-afternoon for the cheaper deals, as the early morning ones go first with the business travellers.

- Travel light. Many budget airlines now charge for bags in the hold, even if you're within your weight limit.

Travel insurance

Another extra cost to add to your holiday bill, but it's worth it. Two things not to skimp on when you're on holiday are sun cream and travel insurance. Compare policies for the level of cover, not just the price.

Here's what you should look for:

- Check the maximum payout. The Association of British Insurers recommend minimum medical cover of one million pounds for Europe and two million worldwide.

- Check the excess in case you need to make a claim. Will you be charged one excess per claim or an excess charge per person *and* per section of the policy you claim under? For example, if you're mugged and lose your passport, will you be clobbered for two excess charges, one for your medical claim and one for your lost passport?

- Always tell your insurer about any 'pre-existing' medical conditions. That's your ongoing back problem, recent operation on your foot and any medication you're taking. If you don't do this and a recurrent problem plays up abroad, you risk your insurer refusing your claim, which may leave you facing a huge bill.

- Don't make the mistake of thinking you're automatically covered for free healthcare in Europe. The EHIC (European Health Insurance Card), which replaced the old E111 form, only entitles you to basic minimum care in European coun-

133

tries and others with reciprocal arrangements with the UK. But we're talking *basic minimum care*, which won't extend to covering the cost of your family staying on if you're hospitalised, or air ambulances home. An air ambulance back from the Canaries could cost around £30,000, so forking out for annual travel cover is well worth it.

- Some packaged bank accounts (the ones you pay a fee for) include *free* travel insurance, but check the limits before relying on it. You may be covered for medical claims but does it cover your luggage, passport and money?

Sue's savvy stories – it happened to me

Sometimes you need to fight your case for an insurance claim, as I did when my camera was stolen in Fiji. It's actually a great story and truth be known the entertainment factor (particularly in the local police station) almost made up for the loss of the camera. I say almost, but not quite.

Having gone out with friends in their hire car we discovered a small local bar well off the beaten track late at night. Rather than come across as being a camera-waving tourist we made what we thought was a sensible decision to leave the camera hidden in an old rucksack in the locked boot of the car.

And, yes, you can guess what happened; an hour later we returned to find the boot broken into and the camera gone.

Three hours spent in the very basic local police station the next day resulted in nothing more than a good old chat about the royal family and being offered copious amounts of 'kava' (the local brew), which unfortunately tastes just like dirty dishwater complete with gritty bits.

The long and short of it was that on returning to the UK with a very basic police report the insurers wouldn't cough up, claiming the camera had been left unattended, which wasn't covered on the policy.

I pointed out that if I'd taken the camera with me and been mugged for it, they'd be facing a claim for not only the camera loss but possibly rather large hospital bills too, hence my calculated decision to leave it in the car. They then rapidly came back with an offer which I rejected, sending them details of the camera's current replacement price. And what do you know, they finally coughed up, minus the £50 excess; sending through a cheque for around £250.

So you don't ask; you don't get.

Get more for your money

Here are a few insider tips on how to get those really cheap flights, upgrades, the VIP lounge and airport parking...

- Get free flights by applying for a new credit card. Some airline-backed credit cards offer free flights when you sign up. All you need to do is apply, spend on the card (in some cases there's no minimum spend), pay off the bill and you'll get a voucher for a free return flight to Europe. Then cut up the card and apply for another one.

- To find the best seats, go to www.airlinequality.com for passenger reviews and the all-important rows and numbers to ask for at check-in. Seat size, along with the amount of legroom, varies according to the airline – at www.seatguru.com you can check each airline's seat size before booking.

- Fly as a courier to get cheap airline tickets. Fares vary according to where you're going, but rest assured all you're carrying is paperwork. Contact airlines for details. If you're travelling as a couple, you can take advantage of one reduced fare, buy the other standard price and you should still be able to check in and sit together.

- It goes without saying that the best seats will be first class – but if you can't afford the fare, join the airline's frequent flyer club as you'll have more chance of an upgrade if you're a 'loyal' customer. Ask at check-in if you can be listed as 'SFU', that's airline speak for 'suitable for upgrade' which gives the impression you're a regular flyer who's been upgraded before.

- Stressed and hassled before you've even boarded the plane? Relax in the executive lounge first; there are over one hundred tucked away in airports across the world, and while it costs from around £13 a time, once in you can enjoy unlimited food and drink. So that could be a glass of champagne before your flight, or a leisurely breakfast reading the complimentary papers. Go to www.loungepass.com for reservations and locations.

Last-minute shopping

Buy sun cream and paperbacks at the supermarket before you go. Stocking up at the airport usually costs more. Price-match your favourite perfume or tipple in the high street before you hit duty free; some supermarkets offer cut-price deals so you *may* find it's cheaper to buy once you're back home than at the airport. Plus buying and packing those extras before the airport means you will have time to relax rather than embark on a full-scale shopping trip.

Airport parking

Don't turn up and park on the day as you'll pay more. Pre-book your space online for the biggest discount: www.gosimply.com/airport-parking and www.holidayextras.co.uk are great sites for savings. Or book an overnight stay at a hotel near the airport; many offer free parking while you're away and a night's accommodation will be much cheaper than two weeks' parking.

Hotels

You don't have to pay the price in the brochure; there are usually deals available if you know what to ask for, and when is the best time to stay.

- Midweek is usually cheaper than weekends, or go for Sunday and Monday rather than the traditional Friday/Saturday break to get a discount.

- Ask about the business rates, which are usually cheaper than the standard charge, though you'll probably have to show a business card for this one.

- Turn up late in the day. Arrive around 4–6pm and if there are rooms left the hotel will be keen to 'sell' them rather than have them sitting empty, so ask for a discount. I did this in a fabulous hotel in Chichester recently, and got £40 off the price of double room.

Car hire

Hiring a car saves you relying on the local transport and it's a great way to explore off the beaten track, but watch out for those hidden costs.

- Price-match and book your car before leaving home. Don't blindly go with the 'big boys' like Hertz, Avis or Thrifty.

- Use websites like www.travelsupermarket.com to compare car hire prices or spend a few minutes doing your own quotes online. Watch for added extras like baby seats and additional drivers, which may not be included in the basic price.

- Book the smallest car you feel able to cope with; the reason being that these get booked first so you'll often find you're upgraded to a bigger model for free. This has happened to me on at least two occasions recently, in Gran Canaria and Tunisia.

- Don't get caught out with petrol costs. You'll be expected to come back with the same amount in the tank as when you started, so if the needle's on the red when you leave the airport make sure that's written on the paperwork so you won't be charged for a full tank at penalty price when you return.

- Collision Damage Waiver (CDW) is the insurance you usually get with the car to cover the bulk of the cost in the event of a prang. But read the small print as you could still be liable for the excess, typically up to £1,000. 'Damage' could be something as simple as scratched paintwork, yet some companies will try to impose the full excess for this. Protect against the risk of forking out for this excess with Damage Excess Waiver. It's an 'optional extra' but is sold under different names including Super Cover, Reimbursement Excess and Car Hire Excess, and often pushed (at a high price) when you collect your car abroad. Buy before you fly; it costs around £2 a day with www.carhireexcess.com and you can find other companies offering similar cover online.

All-inclusive deals

These sound great if there's unlimited food and drink on offer and it saves you scrabbling around for small change when you want a drink by the pool, but check exactly what's included. Some deals only cover certain drinks, usually the local spirits and beers. I've come across deals where just the drinks are 'all inclusive', not the food, so check before you sign up.

If you find the sun saps your hunger, paying for an all-inclusive holiday may not be the best deal for you. Work out roughly what you'd spend on food and drink in a week, based on the local prices, and compare it with the extra you'll pay for an all-inclusive deal.

Holidays from hell

Dirty rooms, inedible food, the pool dug up at three in the morning or the promised sea view visible only through a pair of binoculars.

When it comes to holiday nightmares there's no shortage of people willing to tell their stories of hideous holidays, but not all of them are justified. Complaining that your favourite brand of tomato ketchup wasn't available or that the local bar didn't have the selection of bottled beers you might get at home just won't wash. So b*efore* you complain, think about whether it's really justified. If you feel it is, here's what to do next.

Complain as soon as possible

Don't wait until you're home. Give the hotel, airline or tour operator a chance to fix the problem by telling them as soon as possible.

Sue's savvy stories – it happened to me

Here's an example of why saying something quickly and politely gets a swift and happy result.

While in New York we stayed at the fabulous Hudson Hotel. On the second night the people next door had a late-night party and despite knocking on the door and calling reception it seemed nobody could get them to shut up. So next morning hubby (I was still in bed) went to reception, explained the problem and within a couple of minutes they'd arranged for us to swap rooms, upgrade to a suite (at no extra charge), and had a bottle of wine waiting for us with an apology card that evening.

Now if we'd not said anything and just put up with it and fired off a stroppy letter to the hotel once we got home, we'd have had a miserable stay and might have received an apology and maybe an offer of an upgrade *next* time we visited New York; whereas this way they turned us back into happy customers on the spot.

Suggest a solution

Tell them what you want. Let's be honest, if they think they can get away with giving you a free bottle of the local plonk to make up for a grubby room that's probably what they'll do. So say what you want and, unless it's totally unreasonable, you may well get it.

Be realistic with your expectations

If you can't use the pool for a day while it's cleaned you're not going to get a refund on the entire cost of your holiday, *but* what you could ask for is the option to use the pool at another hotel that day.

Gather evidence

If you don't get the result you want, gather as much evidence as you can to strengthen your case when writing to the company on your return. This can be anything from photos showing the state of your room, the hotel kitchens, pool, view from the bedroom window – whatever you need to prove your case. If other people in the hotel have been affected, get their names, addresses and contact numbers so you can all agree to contact the holiday company on your return.

Obviously don't ruin what's left of your holiday by turning super sleuth every waking hour, but having some form of photographic evidence and a copy of any written complaints made in the resort are all useful when fighting your corner once you're home.

Write to the holiday company

Write to the company's head office. I'd always address any complaint to a named managing director or chief executive to make sure it gets to the top. Outline *briefly* the problem and say what you want; so an apology, explanation or compensation. Don't send original documents like holiday booking forms; photocopies are fine or, better still, email the company along with any photos.

Compensation

If you feel you're entitled to compensation because you've had a disappointing holiday, you need to be realistic about how much of your trip was spoilt because of the problem.

So, say you had six days in the hotel before the pool was closed on the last day, then if the hotel couldn't make alternative arrangements for you to use other pools you *could* look to make a case for a day's lost holiday, *not* an entire refund of your week's holiday.

End of the line

If you complain, one trick many holiday companies pull is offering you vouchers to use against the cost of your next holiday. Don't be afraid to turn this down. Return the vouchers, explaining why you don't want to travel with them again, and ask for the compensation payment in the form of a cheque.

Of course they don't have to send you the cash equivalent; they can stick with their original offer and then you've got to decide whether you want to take your complaint further. That's either to the Small Claims Court or via ABTA, if your holiday company is a member.

You can apply to ABTA online and download a form from www.idrs.ltd.uk, which operates the arbitration scheme. You must return your form within nine months of returning from holiday or the problem arising, whichever is the later. Fees vary according to the amount you're claiming, but for claims up to £3,000 it's around £75. Their postal address is: ABTA Ltd, 30 Park Street, London, SE1 9EQ.

There's more about the Small Claims Court in Chapter 5, but if you pursue the ABTA line you should know that any final decision is legally binding. This means you can't reject the ABTA arbitration decision and *then* take your case to the Small Claims Court; it's one or the other.

Buying and selling on eBay

Selling your clutter and unwanted gifts and purchases on internet auction sites beats dragging yourself out of bed on a Sunday morning to do a car boot sale. And if you're a buyer you can pick up some great deals, as many items are sold new or from small traders who don't have a high-street outlet.

While there are many internet auction sites out there, the biggest and most popular is eBay. It's easy and straightforward to use, but while most of us can manage to post a snap and details of what we're selling, there's a real knack to getting the best price and bagging the best bargains.

How to buy and sell successfully

Seventy-seven per cent of us admit to hoarding junk and clutter at home; that's everything from that old yoghurt maker, car magazines and gadgets to the kids' old toys and CDs you never listen to. We've so much junk that we waste the equivalent of an entire room storing it. Work out the potential cost of that 'lost' space and it could easily be over £100,000 in mortgage payments over the life of your loan. So don't waste money hoarding junk at home, or paying one of those self-storage companies to look after it; sell it.

When it comes to buying goods, don't shop on the high street before you've checked the eBay price, as 54 per cent of items sold on eBay are brand new, so you can pick up some great bargains.

Buying

Lots of things on eBay are cheaper than the high-street price, but what you pay depends on what you're buying, its condition and how much in demand it is. Remember Kate Moss's Topshop collection being snapped up and going for hundreds of pounds once the items hit eBay? And Kylie's green 'Chloe' dress that Tesco made a sassy copy of which flew off the shelves and onto eBay?

Always check the shop price first

Some people fall into the habit of buying on eBay for the convenience, which may mean you can pay more than the high-street price. Check if what you want is cheaper from another outlet by doing a quick search on one of the internet price comparison sites like www.kelkoo.co.uk. Let me give you an example: I recently needed a small table-top ironing board; I did a quick search on eBay and found one being advertised as 'buy now' for £8 plus £4 postage, which the seller said was from Ikea. So I went straight to the Ikea website where I found the exact same one selling for £3.99. So I picked one up from the store on my next visit, saving nearly £10.

Don't fall for tricks like sellers flagging up what looks like an expensive RRP (recommended retail price) to make it seem like you're getting more of a bargain. The recommended retail price is just the price the manufacturer suggests an item sells for. Pick up most hardback books, for example, and you'll see an RRP of around £16–20 in the front jacket cover, yet you can often buy them for around half price in the supermarkets.

Read the description carefully

It's easy to get caught up bidding for what *looks* like a great bargain; but read the sales pitch carefully so you're not caught out. Take note of what's *not* written, too. If there's a list of what's *included* in the price, are there items you'd expect to find that are missing from that list? In other words, they're not included. If you're looking at a mobile phone that claims to be boxed, don't assume the charger and instructions will be in there too (unless it's being sold as new); it's worth asking before bidding.

Check measurements and sizes, particularly if sellers are second-guessing the UK size if, say, it's an American label they're selling. Is the item used or new? Unless it's new, always ask the seller about the exact condition before bidding. Saying things like 'good condition' are too vague, as what's good to one person may be pretty poor to another.

Ask specific questions; so if it's a book that's been 'used', ask if there's bent or torn pages or if the spine is creased. When I'm bidding on clothes, unless advertised as new I always ask if there are any 'marks, tears, stains or holes', so they've got to be totally honest about the condition, including the smallest flaws.

Check out the seller

You'd buy from a store that had a good reputation, so check out sellers' credentials before bidding. Read what others say about them on their feedback profile. They'll have a percentage score based on the amount of good or bad comments they've had and you'll be able to see how others rate the quality of their items and the speed of delivery.

Look at how long they've been trading. A 100 per cent positive feedback score looks great, but if they only sell two items a year it just means two out of two buyers were happy.

Are they a trader or private individual?

You may not think this matters, but you've got more rights if the seller is a business trader rather than a private individual. This is because traders have to abide by the Sale of Goods Act, so it strengthens your rights as a buyer. Ways to spot traders include very high feedback, lots of items regularly up for sale and items being sold in a 'shop' on eBay or the seller having 'power status'.

Buying from a trader

If you buy from 'shops' on eBay you get a better deal in terms of your consumer rights. When buying from a trader on the internet you've got more rights than you do in the high street. So what you're buying must be 'as described, 'of satisfactory quality' and 'fit for purpose'. But in addition to this you've got *extra* rights because you're buying online.

Under the Distance Selling Regulations (full details in Chapter 4) you've got a seven-day cooling-off period where you can cancel, regardless of whether the product is faulty or not. You may, however, be liable for return postage costs unless the item is faulty.

If you're buying secondhand goods from a trader, clearly you can't expect them to be brand new, but what you receive should still match the description.

In *some* cases you can forfeit some of your rights when buying secondhand on an internet auction site; for example, if you're offered the chance to view the goods first but decline, for example when buying a car.

Buying from a private seller

You've far less rights in this situation than when buying from a trader.

What you're buying should still match the description, though, so if you're buying a game and the seller claims it's 'new', yet half the pieces are missing and the box is bashed up, you can complain. While you may have a case against the seller, if they don't agree to a refund you may need to apply to PayPal (providing you made payment this way) for this.

Paying by PayPal, which is eBay's preferred method of payment, means you've got more chance of getting a refund – and there's more on that later.

Make sure you check postage costs before buying

Found something priced well below what it's worth? Check the postage or shipping costs, as some unscrupulous sellers try to bump up their profit by substantially overcharging on postage and you may find exactly the same item available for cheaper postage.

Sue's savvy stories – it happened to me

I recently bought a keyring advertised as 'brand new and boxed', with a £3.99 first-class postage charge. When I received it the postage was a mere 52p. As it ended up, the keyring was poor quality, despite being advertised as new, so I returned it for a refund.

- Check postage prices before bidding, especially on goods being sent from overseas.

- Is postage comparable with rates charged by other sellers for similar items?

- If costs are unclear, contact the seller and ask for a price. If they're vague about the cost or don't respond, don't bid.

Find the bargains others miss

A great way to beat your fellow bargain hunters is by deliberately 'misspelling' what you're looking for. This means you can find the bargains everyone else misses when they search using the correct spelling of the product or brand they want.

The website www.goofbay.com has its own misspelling checker to flag up potential eBay bargains, or you can deliberately type in an incorrect spelling yourself to see what comes up. There are other websites you can check for alternative spelling suggestions, too, such as www.fatfingers.com or www.auctionspeller.com.

If the spelling is incorrect, do check the item being sold is original. It is worth messaging the seller first, to make sure that what they're selling and what you *think* they're selling are one and the same thing.

To find items with no bids, go to www.auctionfinal.com; and if you're after a specific item but can't find it, put details in the 'favourite search' option on eBay and you'll get a message if the item comes up for sale.

Bidding

Don't miss out on bargains because someone pips you to the post.

As a buyer you enter your bid and the maximum you're prepared to pay. Once you've put in that maximum amount the eBay system puts in your bids up to this amount. To stand the best chance of winning, avoid round-number bids as your maximum, such as £4.50 or £10.00, which other people may go for; you'll stand more chance of being successful if you try more obscure bids, such as £5.73 or £7.03.

Sniper bidding

Almost a third of bids happen during the last five minutes of an auction, and it's frustrating to watch online when you're pipped to the post in the final seconds by a higher bidder.

There are now websites that will enter your bids in the closing seconds of the auction. Go to www.goofbay.com and type in what you're bidding for and your maximum price; it will then enter that bid in the final closing seconds, so other bidders aren't alerted to your bids beforehand. It's a free service, though you'll need to register your details on the site first.

Stay local

With large items you'll often be expected to collect in person, which should be flagged up with the item description. But you can cut your postage costs by asking to collect items whenever the seller lives locally.

Message the seller prior to bidding to ask if they're happy for you to do this if you're the highest bidder. They may not always agree, but it is worth asking as it can save you money on post and packing. Depending on the potential postage cost, arranging to collect can make the difference between a good deal and a poor deal.

A handy website to help you out is www.localbargainfinder.co.uk, where you type in your postcode, what you're after and how far you're prepared to go for it and it comes up with a potential list of booty in your area.

Selling

Using the most basic selling style on eBay is free if you list items with a start price of 99p or less, so it is well worth it – even as a last-ditch attempt to sell before you give items to the charity shop or take them to the dump.

How to get the best price

- Look up what you're selling to see how much it's going for and how others describe it; there is nothing to stop you pinching the best bits of their sales blurb.

- Choose the right category under which to list your item. Type in what you're selling and the eBay system automatically suggests the most suitable one. This means your item gets maximum exposure. Otherwise it's a bit like hiding something at the back of a shelf in a shop; if nobody can find it they won't buy it.

- Remember you're 'selling', so talk up your product. Be honest, but there's no harm talking about the 'gorgeous beading' or saying who the item would be good for.

- Take time to write a snappy title with good keywords. Don't just stick to the make and model; include related keywords to pull in more buyers. So if you're selling a handbag, put in words like 'beach', 'office' or 'wedding', so if buyers are searching for a bag for a particular occasion they'll find yours.

- Go for the lowest starting price you can to attract bidders; research has shown a starting price of 99p or less attracts a third more bids than higher starting prices.

And, perhaps most importantly …

Take good clear photos

Check out some of the photos and you'll see a mix of some truly appalling photos and some very professional ones. Taking a good photo can make the difference between getting a good price or not selling at all. Bad photos or, worse still, no photo at all will just make buyers suspicious.

Use a digital camera and take time positioning your item. Photograph it against a plain background so nothing detracts from it. Having something in the background, like a reflection, or taking a snap against a patterned carpet, just won't cut it if you want top price for your item. One eBay insider once told me he always uses a white towel as a background as it photographs well.

Likewise if you're selling clothes, don't take a snap of someone modelling the item but with their head cut off or their legs stuck in a pair of shoes; it just looks naff. Arrange the item of clothing on a mannequin dummy, if you've got one; if not, on a plain wooden (not wire) hanger hung against a plain background.

Personally I always photograph items against the wood floor (unless they're clothes, in which case I hang them up), as it gives a clean, light, neutral background. Take snaps with the flash both on and off to see what works best and always take time to put them on eBay the right way up. You'll lose buyers if they've got to crane their neck sideways to see your picture and if you don't use a 'gallery' picture (that's the small thumbnail snap you see beside the headline description of the item).

When to list your items

It is worth thinking about optimum auction *ending* times before you start. You may find it easier to list your items after lunch on a Monday afternoon, but this might mean that the auction will end at the same time of day so you could lose lots of last-minute opportunist bidders. You can, however, opt for your listing to go 'live' at a fixed time if you're not around then.

According to eBay, the highest number of users is on Sundays, so if you start a ten-day listing on a Thursday evening this gives you two weekends' worth of potential trade, ending on a Sunday evening.

Protect yourself

This is about making sure you get paid, if you're the seller; and if you're buying, that you get what you pay for.

Pay by PayPal

PayPal is owned by eBay and it is the recommended way to make payment. PayPal is basically a secure electronic method of sending money around the world and can be used by both consumers and businesses. You can send and receive money from around two hundred countries across the world, regardless of currency.

Setting up an account is simple and you can do this via the PayPal website. Once the account is up and running, you can send money or get paid directly into your PayPal account. Funds can then be transferred from your PayPal account to your personal bank account.

PayPal protection for buyers

If goods don't arrive, are damaged or are not as described you can apply to PayPal for a refund, including postage costs. In the first instance contact the seller (via eBay) to see if the problem can be resolved amicably. If it can't, you should 'raise' a dispute through PayPal within 45 days of making payment. You've then got another 20 days to raise this dispute to 'claim' level if there's still no favourable response from the seller.

There's no minimum or maximum limit to the amount you can claim through the PayPal protection scheme and the scheme is available free to all buyers.

PayPal protection for sellers

As a seller you can claim against PayPal for missing goods, providing you've got proof you sent them to the buyer's confirmed PayPal address.

You'll get a warning note if the address given for dispatch is different from the one registered with PayPal. If this is the case, contact the buyer to check which address they want the goods sent to and, providing there's some proof of this exchange, you'll be covered under the seller protection policy if there's a problem.

What to watch out for

Although they only affect a very small percentage of the millions of deals done on eBay, there are some fakers and fraudsters out there. While these tend to be clamped down on quickly, here's what to watch out for when buying and selling.

Fake bids

Fake or 'shill bidding' happens when sellers ask friends or family to 'bid up' the price on their items; the idea being to boost the final sale price. But it's not allowed and anyone caught doing this can be struck off.

If you're regularly outbid by the same bidder, check their 'history' to see if they regularly bid on this seller's items. To do this, click on their 'user' name to see what they've bought. Fake bidders tend to bid regularly on items from just one seller.

Check the seller's feedback; is it from different users? Lots of positive feedback from the same eBayers *could* be a sign of 'fake' deals.

Counterfeit goods

That old cliché, 'you get what you pay for' is usually true, so it's unlikely you'll unearth serious designer goods for Primark prices. If there are several sellers selling the same item but just one has no bids or a much lower price, be wary. If others have avoided it, is this for a reason?

- Read listings carefully; spelling mistakes on designer brands *could* indicate items are fake.
- Check the wording; phrases such as 'like' can indicate it's not the real thing. Always email the seller to check the brand if it's unclear; if you don't get a prompt and detailed response, steer clear.

- Watch for CDs, DVDs or video games listed as being bought in Thailand or parts of Asia as they *may* be counterfeit.

Don't fall for bogus emails

These can be anything from suspicious emails asking for your PayPal account details to spoof mails supposedly from eBay claiming they need verification of your account. Never follow the links; log on to your account using the official sites. There'll be information there about where to forward 'spam' mails.

If you get a genuine email from eBay it should appear in the message box of your 'My eBay' section.

Check second-chance offers

You've been outbid but then the seller contacts you with a 'second-chance offer'. This may be genuine if the original buyer pulled out, or it could mean the item was 'bid up' by a friend who's now 'won' so the seller has to offer it elsewhere.

- Email the seller and ask why the original bid fell through – is the reason plausible?
- Stick with the eBay system; don't act on personal emails or being contacted 'out of the blue' by a trader.